LATERAL
LOGIC

PUZZLE YOUR WAY TO
SMART THINKING

Dr Gareth Moore is the creator of daily brain-training site **BrainedUp.com**, and author of a wide range of brain-training and puzzle books for both children and adults, including both *Anti-Stress Puzzles* and *The Brain Workout*.

He gained his Ph.D at the University of Cambridge, where he worked on machine intelligence.

LATERAL
LOGIC

PUZZLE YOUR WAY TO
SMART THINKING

DR GARETH MOORE

Michael O'Mara Books Limited

First published in Great Britain in 2016 by
Michael O'Mara Books Limited
9 Lion Yard
Tremadoc Road
London SW4 7NQ

A CIP catalogue record for this book is available from the British Library.

Papers used by Michael O'Mara Books Limited are natural, recyclable
products made from wood grown in sustainable forests. The
manufacturing processes conform to the environmental regulations of
the country of origin.

ISBN: 978-1-78243-579-2 in paperback print format
ISBN: 978-1-78243-689-8 in ebook format

3 5 7 9 10 8 6 4 2

www.mombooks.com

www.drgarethmoore.com

Typeset and designed by Gareth Moore

Printed and bound by CPI Group (UK) Ltd, Croydon, CR0 4YY

Contents

Introduction

Welcome to *Lateral Logic*! This book contains ninety separate challenges, each designed to get your brain thinking in new and imaginative ways. By the time you've worked your way to the end, you'll have proven yourself a master of both creative thinking and abstract thought!

Puzzle contents
The tasks in this book are broken into three difficulties: beginner, experienced and expert. Even if you're familiar with lateral-thinking puzzles, it's best to start at the beginning and work your way through because many of the questions build on one another as the book progresses. If you jump straight to the end then you'll risk spoiling the solution to a few of the earlier tasks.

There are ninety separate tasks in this book, thirty per difficulty level, each containing an average of two puzzles. Puzzles on the same page are usually related, either in terms of topic or by forming a series of progressive challenges. As with the book in general, it's best to start with the first puzzle on a page before trying the second, so as not to spoil the answer to the preceding puzzle.

Some of the tasks in this book are designed to help you build your lateral-thinking skills by providing carefully constrained creative challenges. These will aid in unlocking creative abilities innate to all of us that you might not have realized you have!

Hints and solutions
On the reverse side of each puzzle page you'll find both a 'Hints' section and a 'Solutions' section. You shouldn't be shy about reading the 'Hints' if you get stuck on a puzzle, but start with the first hint, if there is more than one, and then return to the puzzle for a bit before you read the second or subsequent hints. The hints

are arranged in order of revelation, from least to most, so the more hints you read then the easier the puzzle will become.

Full solutions are given for every puzzle, but if you aren't sure if you have the expected solution then it's a good idea to read the hints first, even if you don't think you need them, to see if your solution seems to match up. In this way you won't be spoiled for the given solution if you've managed to come up with another answer.

For some lateral-thinking puzzles there may be other reasonable solutions, but it's worth remembering that what you're really looking for in most cases is the simplest, most sensible solution to a puzzle. It's often possible to come up with bizarre and unlikely solutions, so the skill is in finding a clean and realistic answer in each case. It's up to your own judgement as to whether any alternative answer you might find lives up to those criteria.

There are also some puzzles in this book which have specific, unique answers. It will always be clear from the text when you reach this type of task, so in these cases the answer given is the only correct solution.

How to solve lateral-thinking puzzles
Lateral-thinking puzzles typically require you to think about options which are not specifically given in the question. A classic example involves a hypothetical situation where there are three light bulbs in one room and three switches in another. You are told that each light switch operates a different one of the three bulbs, but what you don't know is which switch is which. All of the bulbs are switched off, and you can't see the room with the bulbs from the room where the switches are. The problem is to work out which switch controls which bulb, without entering

either room more than once. You are on your own in the rooms, so you can't just call out to someone else to see which bulb is affected by which switch.

If you were able to go in and out of each room twice, the problem would be simple. You would enter the room with the switches, turn on one switch, go to the room with the bulbs and make a note of which bulb had illuminated. You'd then return to the switch room and turn on a second switch, before returning again to the room with the lights and seeing which bulb had come on the second time. Clearly, the third switch would then control the third bulb, and the problem would be solved.

You only have a single visit to the switch room, so you must do something else to allow you to identify which bulb each of the three switches controls. To solve the puzzle, it's best to start by thinking through all of the possibilities, which seem to be:

1) Turn on no switches
2) Turn on one switch
3) Turn on two switches
4) Turn on all three switches

Option 1 won't help, since you will clearly learn nothing. Option 2 will identify one switch-bulb pair, but leave you with a 50:50 guess for the other two. Similarly, option 3 will identify the off bulb as corresponding to one of the switches, but again leave you with a 50:50 guess for the remaining two switches. Option 4 is no better than option 1.

In an ordinary type of puzzle, one of the four options above would be the answer, because in a non-lateral-thinking puzzle you tend to have all the possible parameters explicitly given to you in the question. In this case, however, you need to think of options which are *not* explicitly given to you. Once you do this, of course, there are often many different potential solutions, as discussed above, but what you're always looking for is the easiest and most reasonable solution.

In this particular puzzle, if the question hadn't mentioned that you were on your own then an easy solution would simply have been to have a second person in the bulb room, and to call out to them as you toggle each switch on and off. That person wouldn't have been explicitly mentioned in the question, but you would have thought laterally about how you would be able to solve the puzzle using more than just the information and ideas directly given to you in the question.

You might also come up with a complex way of solving this puzzle, such as perhaps installing a video camera in the bulb room and then turning on the three switches one at a time, followed by watching the video recording back to see which bulb came on in which order. That's a perfectly reasonable solution, although it's more complex than the solution given below so subjectively it's not quite as good. Another reasonable but more complex solution would be to install a series of mirrors so that you can see from one room to the other. Short of adding a huge number of conditions to every lateral-thinking question, it's rarely possible to exclude all other potential answers.

Having exhausted options with the switches, what this puzzle now requires you to do is to think about the bulbs instead of the switches. To give you a hint, if you are now told that the solution does not involve any additional equipment, but does require you being able to reach the bulbs, can you make any progress?

You're explicitly told that the room contains *light bulbs*, rather than some nondescript light source. This is important, because the intended solution might not be possible if you were using some more modern types of lighting. So the question becomes, is there some property of the bulbs which you can use to solve the puzzle, other than simply whether they are emitting light or not?

The solution, if you haven't yet thought of it, relies on the fact that bulbs get hot when they're switched on. Therefore you simply turn on two light switches and wait a while to give the bulbs a chance to heat up. You then turn off one of the light switches and move to the room with the bulbs. At this point you have three bulbs in three different states: on; off but hot; and off but not hot. You can use this to pair the bulbs with their corresponding switches. Solved!

Now you've seen how that puzzle works, try this one:

There are a dozen or so identical coins on a table, and you decide to show a magic trick to your friend. You ask her to take one of the coins and write her initials on one side of it with a marker, then squeeze it tightly in her fist 'to make sure the initials are firmly impressed into the coin'. Having run through some standard magician-type patter, you then ask her to put the coin back on the table, upside-down so as to conceal her initials, and then shuffle the coins while you aren't looking. You are then able to locate her coin from those on the table, without turning any of them over. How do you do it?

The solution is very similar to the previous puzzle, requiring you to use a property of the coin that is not immediately obvious. You could try to second-guess where your friend may have put the coin, or come up with some complex mechanical or electronic way of tracking the coin, but the solution is beautifully simple.

You just touch each coin in turn until you find the one that is hotter than the rest, since it has been held tightly in her fist while you talked, and that's her coin. If you try this trick in real life it will be much easier if you make sure the coins rest in a cold room for a while prior to the trick! But as a lateral-thinking puzzle, it requires you to again think about something that isn't explicitly mentioned in the question, and to use it to find a perfectly reasonable and sensible solution to the puzzle.

Now you've seen two example puzzles, you're well prepared to get started on the actual puzzles. And if you happen to find solutions that you think are better than those given, or equally as good, feel free to let me know by emailing gareth@braincdup.com – if they're good enough then they might be given as alternative answers in any future edition of the book!

Dr Gareth Moore

Puzzle 1 – Beginner

Lateral thinking involves, as the name suggests, thinking about things from a different perspective to that which you would normally use in everyday life – or *laterally*, in other words.

Try this first teaser:

Is it legal for a man to marry his widow's sister?

(handwritten: man is dead)

?

Hints

Like all of the puzzles in this book, there are solving hints at the top of the following page. These are broken down into a series of steps, each becoming more specific in turn. If you get stuck on a puzzle, read just the first bulleted hint and then return to the puzzle. Only read the later hints if you still need them.

Solutions

A solution is also given at the bottom of the following page, again as per all following pages in this book. In some cases there is one correct solution, but other times what is given is simply a perfectly reasonable answer – for some lateral-thinking puzzles there may be other sensible answers, as well as many outlandish ones too!

Lateral Warm-up
Puzzle 1 – Hints

- Is this a problem that can ever occur?

- Are you sure the question makes sense?

- Think about the status of the man.

Lateral Warm-up
Puzzle 1 – Solutions

It isn't legal, because the man would be dead – otherwise he wouldn't have a widow!

The lateral thinking involved in solving this puzzle is simply to realize that the question is deliberately misleading you. To solve it, you need to take a step back and think about what precisely you're being asked.

Thinking It Through

Try this lateral-thinking puzzle, which requires you to connect together a couple of pieces of knowledge to reach a definite conclusion:

An explorer builds a house on a particular spot where all sides of the house have fantastic southern views. From one window she can see a bear.

What colour is the bear?

[handwritten notes in left margin: must be in North Pole ∴ Polar bear → white]

[handwritten notes in right margin: all sides can't face south]

Now try this second teaser:

A window cleaner is standing on a ledge to clean the windows on the twentieth floor of a large skyscraper. He's high above the ground, when all of a sudden a strong gust of wind causes him to lose his balance and he falls off the ledge.

[handwritten note in left margin: he's indoor]

He is not fastened to the ledge and falls freely, yet survives without injury. How is this possible? There are no balconies or other sticking-out structures on the building.

See overleaf for hints to both puzzles.

Bear

- Where in the world must the house be for this to be true?

- So what sort of bear must be visible from the house?

Window Cleaner

- Where exactly is the window cleaner standing?

- He falls off a ledge thanks to a gust of wind, but where is the ledge?

Thinking It Through
Puzzle 2 – Solutions

Bear

The bear is white. The house must be at the North Pole, so she must be looking at a polar bear, which are always white.

Window Cleaner

The window cleaner is cleaning the inside of the window. He is standing on a raised ledge, and the gust of wind blew in through an open window pane. He falls just a couple of feet to the floor below, so is not injured.

Puzzle 3 – Beginner

In a particular society the following rule applies to all women:

You can have as many children as you like,
until you bear a male baby. At that point
you may have no further children.

Question

How does this rule affect the overall balance of male and female children in that society?

50 | 50
- You should assume that male and female children have exactly the same chance of being born, for any given birth.

- You should also assume that no other external factors apply to influence the answer in any way.

See overleaf for hints.

Baby Births
Puzzle 3 – Hints

- There is equal chance of any one baby being a boy or a girl. So if all parents only wanted one child, this policy would have no effect at all.

- What if all parents want two children? How does this affect the overall relative numbers of boys and girls?

- If all children are equally likely to be born as a boy or as a girl, what does this tell us about how the policy will affect the overall balance of genders in society? If you look at just one birth, does it affect it? What about two, three, four or even five births?

Baby Births
Puzzle 3 – Solutions

The policy has no effect on the overall gender balance, because it does not change the likelihood that any particular baby is born as a boy or as a girl. Some parents get to have more children if they wish, but the chance of each child being either a boy or a girl remains the same, so overall there will remain on average an equal number of boys and of girls in that society. It's easy to confuse the effect it will have on some parents with the effect on society.

Puzzle 4 – Beginner

Try these teasers:

1

David's mother has three children. The first child is called **May** and the second is called **June**. What is the **third** child called?

1st May
2nd June
3rd David

_____

2

Can you name three consecutive days (in English!) without mentioning Saturday, Sunday or Wednesday?

- Christmas Eve
- Christmas Day
- Boxing Day

Puzzle 4 – Hints

1

- The answer is not July!

- There is a definite answer.

2

- What other days are there?

- Can you name some days, other than specific weekdays?

Nominative Determination
Puzzle 4 – Solutions

1

The answer is given in the question, if you read it again. It's David.

2

Yesterday, today and tomorrow. Or you could name three specific dates, or even three days that always appear in succession such as Christmas Eve, Christmas Day and Boxing Day.

Black-out Austen

Puzzle 5 – Beginner

Black out some of the words in this extract from *Pride and Prejudice*, so what's left forms a very short story of your own invention. This is a great 'creative thinking' task, suitable even for people who think they 'can't be creative'! Use a bold, black marker if you can, so it's really clear which words still remain. *See overleaf for an example.*

Not all that Mrs Bennet, however, with the assistance of her five daughters, could ask on the subject, was sufficient to draw from her husband any satisfactory description of Mr Bingley. They attacked him in various ways – with barefaced questions, ingenious suppositions, and distant surmises; but he eluded the skill of them all, and they were at last obliged to accept the second-hand intelligence of their neighbour, Lady Lucas. Her report was highly favourable. Sir William had been delighted with him. He was quite young, wonderfully handsome, extremely agreeable, and, to crown the whole, he meant to be at the next assembly with a large party. Nothing could be more delightful! To be fond of dancing was a certain step towards falling in love; and very lively hopes of Mr Bingley's heart were entertained.

"If I can but see one of my daughters happily settled at Netherfield," said Mrs Bennet to her husband, "and all the others equally well married, I shall have nothing to wish for."

In a few days Mr Bingley returned Mr Bennet's visit, and sat about ten minutes with him in his library. He had entertained hopes of being admitted to a sight of the young ladies, of whose beauty he had heard much; but he saw only the father. The ladies were somewhat more fortunate, for they had the advantage of ascertaining from an upper window that he wore a blue coat, and rode a black horse.

An invitation to dinner was soon afterwards dispatched; and already had Mrs Bennet planned the courses that were to do credit to her housekeeping, when an answer arrived which deferred it all. Mr Bingley was obliged to be in town the following day, and, consequently, unable to accept the honour of their invitation, etc.

Not sure how to start? Just pick some words to cross out or leave in, and get started! You can even cross out just part of a word if you wish.

Here's an example:

~~Not all that~~ Mrs Ben~~net, however, with the assistance of her five daughters, could ask on the subject,~~ was sufficient to ~~draw from her~~ husband ~~any satisfactory description of~~ Mr Bing~~ley. They attached him~~ in various ways – ~~with barefaced questions, ingenious suppositions, and distant surmises,~~ but he eluded the ~~skill of them all, and they were at last obliged to accept the~~ second-hand intelligence of ~~their neighbour, Lady Lucas. Her report was highly favourable.~~ Sir Will~~iam had been delighted with him.~~ He was quite ~~young, wonderfully~~ handsome, extremely ~~agreeable, and, to crown the whole, he meant to be at the next assembly with a~~ large ~~party. Nothing could be more delightful! To be fond of dancing was a certain step towards falling in love,~~ and very lively ~~hopes of Mr Bingley's heart were entertained~~.

"~~If~~ I can ~~but see one of my daughters~~ happily settle~~d at Netherfield,"~~ ~~said Mrs Bennet to~~ her husband~~, "and all the others equally well married,~~ I ~~shall~~ have no~~thing to~~ wish for."

In a ~~few days Mr Bingley~~ returned ~~Mr Bennet's~~ visit~~, and sat about ten minutes with him in~~ his ~~library. He had entertained~~ hopes of being ~~admitted to a sight of the~~ young ~~ladies, of whose beauty he had heard much, but he saw only the father. The ladies~~ were somewhat ~~more~~ fortunate, for they ~~had the advantage of ascertaining from an upper window that he~~ wore a blue ~~coat, and rode a black~~ horse.

A~~n invitation to~~ dinner was ~~soon afterwards dispatched, and already had Mrs Bennet~~ planned ~~the courses that were to do credit to her housekeeping,~~ when ~~an answer arrived which deferred it all.~~ Mr Bing~~ley~~ was obliged to ~~be in town the following day, and, consequently, unable to accept the~~ honour ~~of~~ their invitation~~, etc.~~

It Can't Be Wrong

Many lateral-thinking puzzles have no definitive solution. They simply present a strange situation and ask the solver to come up with a plausible explanation. Sometimes these explanations can appear a little far-fetched, but the best lateral-thinking puzzles have at least one solution which, when you finally discover it, fully explains the situation.

Try this version of a classic puzzle:

A man walks into a bar and asks for a glass of water. Instead, the barman suddenly slams a tray on the bar and screams in his face.

Why?

Puzzle 6 – Hints

- What reasons could the man have for wanting a glass of water?

- What effect would suddenly slamming something down and screaming at someone have?

- Was the barman trying to scare him? Why?

- What connects a glass of water and scaring someone?

It Can't Be Wrong

Puzzle 6 – Solutions

The man asked for a glass of water because he had hiccups. The barman realized this and so attempted to cure the hiccups by startling him. He did this by making a loud noise with the tray and then by screaming in his face.

Thinking Both Ways

Puzzle 7 – Beginner

Some puzzles can only be solved by using steps that might not immediately be obvious, or seem counter-intuitive.

One well-known example involves ferrying animals across a river:

cat → chicken
chicken → grain

A farmer has a cat, a chicken and some grain. If left alone, the cat will eat the chicken, and the chicken will eat the grain. He needs to cross a river, but his boat is only large enough to carry one of these at any time. So how does he do it without any of them getting eaten?

If he crosses with the cat, the grain will get eaten, and if he crosses with the grain, the chicken will get eaten. So he must first cross with the chicken. But what does he do next? Once he's gone back and brought the grain or cat next, it will get eaten or eat the other when he goes back for the final item.

→ chicken
→ cat
chicken ←
→ grain

For a further challenge, try this more complex version:

chicken →

A farmer has a big dog, a little dog, a cat, a chicken and some grain. If left alone, the big dog will attack the little dog, the little dog will attack the cat, the cat will attack the chicken and the chicken will eat the grain. He needs to cross a river, but his boat is only large enough to carry two of these at any time. So how does he do it without any of them getting attacked or eaten?

- The first move has to be to bring the chicken over, and then the next move must be to bring either the cat or the grain over – but then what is the next move? Assuming the puzzle has a solution, you can't be stuck at this point. So what do you do next?

- Perhaps you have to undo a previous move.

- Try bringing the chicken back again, even though this may seem both counter-intuitive and inefficient. In fact, there is no way of avoiding it.

Thinking Both Ways

The solution is not immediately obvious because it involves undoing a step you have already done:
First, bring over the chicken
Return empty, then bring over the cat.
Return *with the chicken*, then bring over the grain.
Return empty, then bring over the chicken.
This also works if you bring over the grain before the cat.

For the second version, you need a similar reversal step too:
Bring over the little dog and the chicken.
Return empty, then bring over the big dog and grain.
Return with the little dog and the chicken, then bring over the cat.
Return empty, then bring over the little dog and chicken.

Puzzle 8 – Beginner

1

You're staying in a remote holiday home and it's the dead of night. The lights go out and can't be restored. You have only a candle, some firewood and also an oil lamp. You only have one match, so what should you light first?

_____

2

You're staying in a remote holiday home and the lights are all out. You have no way of making the lights come back on, nor any other way of generating light. And yet you are still able to see your way around the house perfectly. You don't own night-vision goggles or anything similar, so how is this possible?

It's daytime

1

- Pretend you're actually doing it. What would you really light first?

- You pick up the match, and then you light ... what?

2

- How would you normally see your way around a house if the lights weren't on?

- What *doesn't* the question mention?

- Does it say what time of day it is?

It's So Obvious

Puzzle 8 – Solutions

1

If you think it through, clearly you would have to light the match first!

2

It is daytime, so no further illumination is required – daylight is shining through the windows.

Pixel Art
Puzzle 9 – Beginner

It's often easier to be 'creative' when you restrict yourself to a more limited set of options. This can also help make it easier to get started.

Shade some of the squares in this frame to make a picture of your own devising. Even if you start entirely at random, you'll probably end up getting inspired at some point!

Activities such as this one are similar to lateral thinking, since you need to make creative use of the limited resources you have.

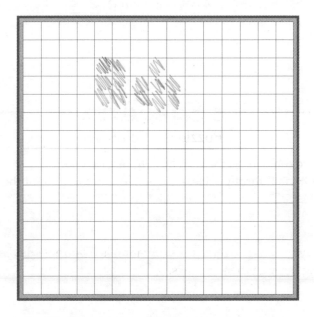

Pixel Art

Puzzle 9 – Hints

- There's no wrong answer here. You could create a pattern, perhaps, or just shade some random squares and see what it looks like – you might be surprised!

- If you want to draw something specific, it's probably best to pick something easily recognizable, such as a face.

Pixel Art

Puzzle 9 – Solutions

Here are some ideas that might help inspire you!

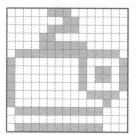 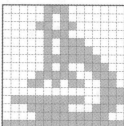 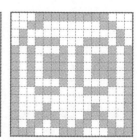

Joined-up Thinking
Puzzle 10 – Beginner

Here's a problem that seems impossible, but is in fact perfectly solvable.

Can you use a pen to join these three circles with a single straight line, without lifting the pen from the book?

To be precise, can you place a ruler flat down on the book such that a line drawn along the edge of that ruler will pass through each of these three shaded circles?

- If you start from the assumption that the puzzle isn't lying and it does indeed have a solution, then this helps. If your initial belief is that it is, nonetheless, impossible, then one of your assumptions must be wrong. Which one?

- You can't lift the pen or the ruler, so what else can you manipulate to make this possible?

- Can you do something to the paper?

Joined-up Thinking
Puzzle 10 – Solutions

One method for solving this puzzle is simply to tear strips into the page and then weave them over each other, so you can place the ruler on top of the result and then draw a straight line down.

A less destructive solution is to fold the page like this:

That is, fold the page back so the middle dot is in line with the top and bottom dots. You'll need to nudge in the paper a bit at the bottom, so the ruler/line can cross through the printed dot too.

1

You're taking part in the 1,500 metres race at the Olympics, and as you approach the finish line you overtake the competitor in second place. What place are you in now?

2ⁿᵈ

2

Now you're taking part in the 200 metres sprint at the Olympics, and you've just overtaken the competitor in last position. What place are you currently in?

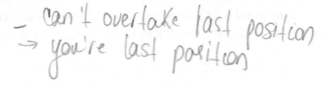

– can't overtake last position
→ you're last position

Race Conditions

1

What's one better than second place? First place, right? So if you overtake the person in second place, are you actually in first place?

2

Can you overtake the person in last position?

Race Conditions

1

When you overtake the person in second place, you're then in second place yourself – not first place!

2

You can't overtake the person in last place in a race because if you were able to overtake them then they couldn't have been in last place! In races where you lap competitors it's arguably possible, however, but this is not the case in the 200 metres at the Olympics.

Picture Posers
Puzzle 12 – Beginner

At first glance, each of the images at the bottom of this page appears to be rather basic. The first is mostly just a circle, and the second is two wavy lines. But with a bit of imagination they can become something else.

You can even explain an empty box:

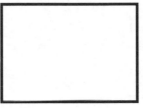

A polar bear in the snow

What creative descriptions can you come up with for each of the following images? There is space beneath each one to write a suitable caption!

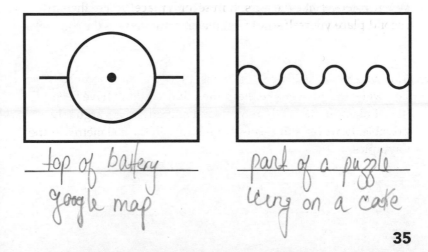

top of battery

google map

part of a puzzle

icing on a cake

If you aren't sure where to start, just think of something each image genuinely looks like, and take it from there.

For example, the first image could be a close-up of a decorated die, or perhaps an eye of some sort.

The second image might be a close-up of a closed zip.

Picture Posers

Puzzle 12 – Solutions

There is obviously no correct answer. For the first image, it could be a person with a very large hat riding a bicycle. The second could be a monster's mouth – just wait until you see the tongue!

Coin Conundrum

Puzzle 13 – Beginner

These nine coins are arranged in a diamond shape.

By moving just two coins, can you change it into a triangular shape?

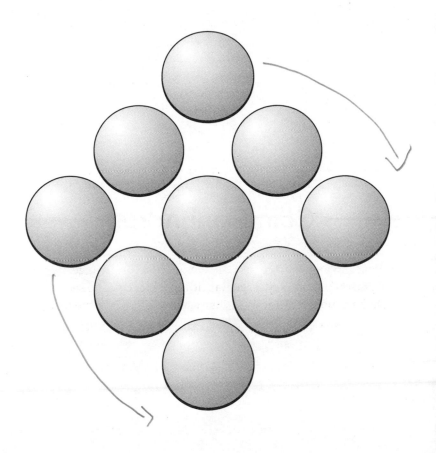

Coin Conundrum

Puzzle 13 – Hints

- The shape is also a rotated square. If you view it rotated through 45 degrees, as a square, does that make it easier?

- It might appear that you need to move three coins to solve this, but perhaps you're not looking at it from a suitable angle?

Coin Conundrum

Puzzle 13 – Solutions

Puzzle 14 – Beginner

1

Which side of a cat contains the most hair?

outside

2

How many birthdays does a typical person have?

1

3

What do you call a bear with its ear cut off?

half deaf? b

Riddle or Joke?

1

Well, which side do you think?

2

It's a matter of how you interpret the question ...

3

This is more of a joke, really – it's based on some wordplay. Can you spot what it might be?

Riddle or Joke?

Puzzle 14 – Solutions

1

The outside, obviously.

2

One. How many birthdays do you have?!

3

A 'B'.

Cake for Eight
Puzzle 15 – Beginner

It's your birthday (hooray!) and you have a circular cake to divide between eight people.

How can you cut it into eight equally sized pieces *with just three straight cuts*?

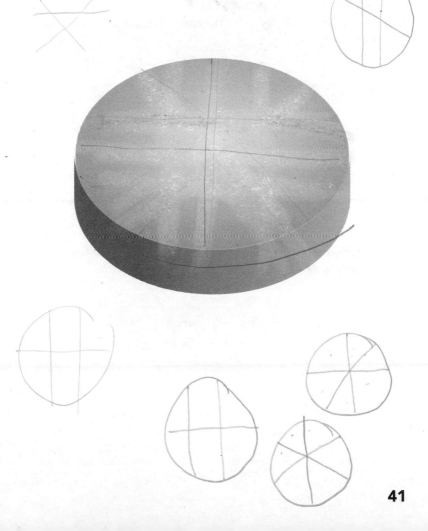

Cake for Eight
Puzzle 15 – Hints

- Draw a circle and see if you can do it in three lines. Remember that the pieces all need to be the same size!

- Is it impossible? Perhaps there is a twist you haven't thought of?

- A literal twist, for example. Is there something you can do with a cake that you can't do with a flat circle?

Cake for Eight
Puzzle 15 – Solutions

Just make two perpendicular cuts top-down, and one horizontal cut through the body of the cake:

1

not married to each other

Karen and Kris have been married for twenty
years and are in love with one another.
Yet when Kris announces he's getting a
divorce, Karen is delighted. Why?

*∟o divorcing his wife
Karen is his mistress.*

2

A couple have three daughters, and each
daughter has one brother. How many
children do they have in total?

3

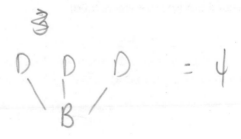

D   D   D   = 4
\ | /
B

1

What doesn't the question say? Might this be relevant?

2

Is this a maths question or a family question?

Family Matters
Puzzle 16 – Solutions

1

Kris is currently married to someone else.

2

Four, since they all share the same brother. It's tempting to treat this as a maths question and add on one brother per sister!

Puzzle 17 – Beginner

Here's another creative challenge for you, which is a good test of your ability to think about and picture things abstractly:

Create a picture by joining some or
all dots using only straight lines.

Lines can only be between the centres of dots, and not between any other point. Despite these restrictions, there's still plenty of opportunity to be creative!

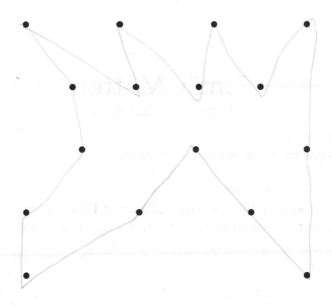

Line Drawing
Puzzle 17 – Hints

- It's quite tricky to envisage something that will actually fit the dot pattern, so the best way to tackle this is just to draw a few random lines and see what it reminds you of at that point.

- You can use the dots as part of the picture too, especially if you don't join lines to them.

Line Drawing
Puzzle 17 – Solutions

There's no specific solution to this challenge, but here's one effort. It's a crazy bird running to the left!

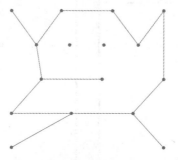

Misdirection
Puzzle 18 – Beginner

You're on an extended hike through a desert-like wilderness. Towns are few and far between, so you are being very careful to always follow the correct path at each junction.

You've just arrived at a crossroads in the path, but unfortunately the signpost here has fallen over and is lying some distance away in the sand. It still points in four directions, but these are now up, down, east and west, and it's obvious that at least the up and down are definitely wrong!

There's nothing about the way the post fits into the ground which shows you which way it originally stood, and yet still you are able to follow the correct junction away from the crossroads.

How?

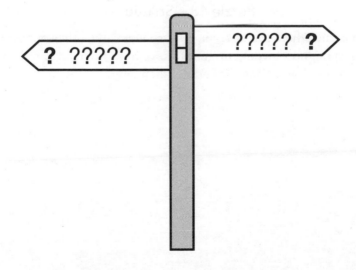

Misdirection

- Try and picture the situation. The signpost is lying on the ground but is otherwise intact.

- Towns are few and far between, so what does this make likely?

- The signpost probably points back where you've come from.

Misdirection

Puzzle 18 – Solutions

You know where you've come *from*, so you can work out which way the signpost would originally have been oriented and then follow it just as well as if it hadn't fallen over.

A Safe Prediction

Puzzle 19 – Beginner

- Think of a number from one to twenty and then triple it.

- Add fifteen to the result.

- Double what you now have.

- Now subtract twelve from the current value.

- Divide by six.

- Now subtract your original number.

- The number you now have is three.

Now here's the question: can you explain why the prediction was correct? Why is the answer always three?

- Try writing this out as a series of mathematical steps, rather than in words.

- Let's call the original number x. What happens to x at each step?

You start with x and then triple it, to give $3x$. Next you add 15, so the result so far is $3x + 15$. Next you double everything, which means your current value is $6x + 30$. If you now subtract 12, you end up with $6x + 18$. The next step is to divide by 6, which gives $x + 3$. The final step is to subtract back off the original number, leaving just 3, the guaranteed answer.

Trapped in Glass
Puzzle 20 – Beginner

There are many different puzzles that could be placed under the general heading of 'matchstick puzzle', but this one is a very good one to start with because it involves very few matches.

The problem seems at once straightforward and yet turns out to be surprisingly tricky, because the solution requires a step that might not be obvious.

Arrange four matchsticks (or pencils, or straws, or any narrow and long objects) as follows, with a coin placed as shown.

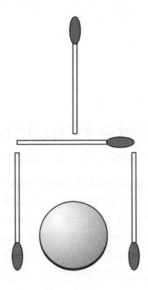

Here's the puzzle: can you move just two matches so that the coin escapes from the 'wineglass', but the wineglass remains *exactly* the same shape?

- Which way do you think the wineglass ends up pointing afterwards?

- Here's a hint: the final wineglass is facing upwards instead of downwards.

- Try with actual matches (or equivalents), and see if you can solve it.

- When you move one of the matches it will only need to travel a short distance.

Trapped in Glass
Puzzle 20 – Solutions

This puzzle is tricky because one of the matches slides just half its length to one side. It's natural to want to move matches to entirely new positions, so this, combined with the fact that the wineglass ends up in a different orientation, can make it hard to find this solution:

Try these puzzles:

1
Which word is always spelled incorrectly?

_____

2
There is a fly in my coffee so I send it back. When it returns, I know the waiter has simply removed the fly and poured it into a new cup. How do I know that?

_____

3
What goes up when rain comes down?

1

Think about the spelling of the words in the puzzle.

2

What might identify the coffee as yours but in such a way that the waiter wouldn't have noticed?

3

Imagine that it's just starting to rain. What goes up?

Try This Trio
Puzzle 21 – Solutions

1

The word 'incorrectly'.

2

You had put sugar or sweetener in it, and can taste it.

3

An umbrella.

Pour Problem
Puzzle 22 – Beginner

In a case of rather poor beverage planning, you have turned up to cater a dinner party without the amount of wine that you promised.

The host, who is particularly fussy about having precise quantities, requires exactly six litres of wine. All you have, however, are three containers, which you know hold exactly two, five and seven litres respectively.

The two- and five-litre containers are empty, but the seven-litre container is full. You also have a funnel that allows you to pour liquid between containers without spilling any.

How can you measure out *precisely* six litres of wine? There is an exact solution to find – doing it 'by eye' is not the solution!

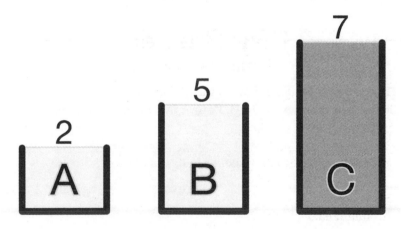

Pour Problem

- Start by pouring from C into B.

- Next, pour from B into A. This leaves 2, 3 and 2 litres in A, B and C respectively.

- So you can now make 4 litres in C by pouring A across.

Pour Problem

Pour C into B for 0-5-2. Pour B into A for 2-3-2. Pour A into C for 0-3-4. Pour B into A for 2-1-4. Pour A into C for 0-1-6, solving the problem.

1

You can see me in the light,
But I vanish in the night.
I only dance when you dance,
And I flicker in candle glance.
I am a version of your might.
What am I?

2

I pass you by on every day,
Always going the same way.
I never arrive at any place,
And sometimes I seem to race,
When you feel me run away.
What am I?

1

- What can you see in light, but vanishes at night?

- What might it be that will 'only dance when you dance'?

2

- What passes by every day?

- What keeps going forever, never arriving anywhere?

- What can sometimes run away from you?

1

Your shadow fits all of these descriptions, since it will flicker in candlelight, and dance when you dance, and is ultimately a projection of you ('version of your might').

2

Time does all of these things, and in particular it is said that time sometimes runs away from you.

Cut It Out

Puzzle 24 – Beginner

For this challenge you'll need a square of paper and a pair of scissors. A small sheet from a memo block is ideal, or otherwise you can simply cut a rectangular sheet of paper into a rough square. You don't need a large sheet of paper – in fact, pretty much any size will do.

The challenge is to reproduce a pattern *only* by repeatedly folding the paper in half, and then making a *single* straight line cut.

You can fold either diagonally or horizontally/vertically, just so long as the paper ends up being exactly half the size after the fold that it was before. The single cut, which is the final step, can be wherever you like, then unfold the paper. For example, you can form a rotated square in the centre of a piece of paper like this:

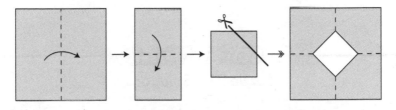

Now work out how to form this result by following these rules:

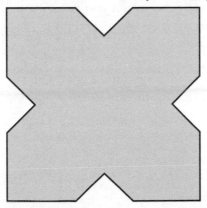

Puzzle 24 – Hints

- You need to end up with diagonal cut-outs, so there needs to be at least one diagonal fold involved somewhere.

- The cut-out areas that appear would require eight cuts if there was no folding, so you must fold it three times (since a single cut will make two cuts in the paper after one fold, four after a second fold, and eight after a third).

- Start by folding diagonally, and then fold diagonally again.

- Now fold again.

- And finally, make a cut – it's up to you to work out where!

Cut It Out

Puzzle 24 – Solutions

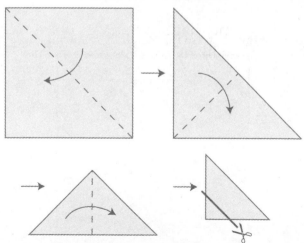

1

If I dig a square hole into the mud that is 3 metres wide by 3 metres long, and 5 metres deep, what is the volume of mud in the hole?

2

A mother has two children, at least one of whom is a boy. Without knowing the gender of the other child, what is the probability that she actually has two boys?

Assume that boys and girls are equally likely to have been born.

1

- Imagine that you've just dug the hole out.

- How much mud is in the hole?

2

- The question is *not* 'What is the chance that the woman's *next* child is a boy?', which would be 1 in 2, or a half. So what exactly is the question asking?

- What would the likelihood be that she has two boys, if you didn't already know that she had at least one boy?

Mystery Numbers
Puzzle 25 – Solutions

1

There's no mud in the hole, since you've already dug it out!

2

It's 1 in 3, or a third. You might expect it to be 1 in 2, or a half, because after all you already know she has a boy, but that would be the answer to the question 'If she had another child, what is the likelihood of it being a boy?'. The fact is she *already has* the two children, so you need to look at the probability that she has two boys. Without any other information, the possibilities are boy-boy, boy-girl, girl-boy and girl-girl, meaning she would have a 1 in 4, or a quarter, chance of two boys. But we can eliminate girl-girl, so the chance she has two boys is now 1 in 3, or a third.

Rhyme the Line

Not everyone is a poet, but you can surely think of at least one word that rhymes with almost any other word.

Now take that innate ability to the next level, by writing just one line to form a complete two-line poem. Whoever said that poems needed to be long?

For example, given the line:
Each morning I awake with glee,
... you could perhaps follow it with the rhyming line:
Yearning for a cup of tea.

See what you can come up with for each of these examples:

1.
Throughout the year I wake and say,

_____

2.
If I could have just one more thing,

_____

Rhyme the Line

- Start by thinking of some words that rhyme with the last word of the given line.

- Do any of these words seem to fit in any way with the first line?

- It doesn't matter if the connection is ridiculous – this often makes it funnier, which is usually a good thing when it comes to two-line poems!

Rhyme the Line

Puzzle 26 – Solutions

There is of course no correct solution. Here are two suggestions:

1.
Throughout the year I wake and say,
I wish it were still Saturday!

2.
If I could have just one more thing,
I'd wish for twenty more, and win!

1

A man pushed his car along until he reached a hotel, whereupon he stopped. At that exact moment he realized he was bankrupt.
Why?

2

You look out of the window and you see that a carrot, a scarf and some stones are lying in the middle of the road.
Why?

Explain These

1

When have you ever pushed a car along? You might even have done this as a kid.

2

What might have caused these to be left there? Could something else have been there too that is now gone?

Explain These

1

The man is playing *Monopoly*, and he has just landed on a property with a hotel that has a rent he cannot afford to pay, so he is bankrupt and out of the game.

2

There was previously snow over the road and a snowman had been built there. Now it has melted, just its eyes (stones), nose (carrot) and scarf remain.

What's in the Box?

Look at this empty box. There's something sticking out of it on all four sides, but what do you think is actually *inside* the box?

Grab a pencil, and draw in what you think might be inside.

There's no correct answer – the idea is just to stir your creative juices, which you'll need to solve some of the lateral-thinking puzzles in this book!

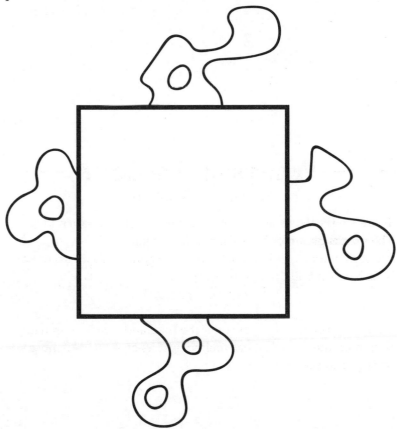

What's in the Box?

- It looks a bit like that mess you get when you pour too little pancake batter into a frying pan!

- They look a bit like tentacles too, maybe.

- Are those circles eyes or holes, or something else altogether?

What's in the Box?

There's no correct solution, but this idea maybe looks a bit like a genie that just came out of a lamp ...

Hobson's Choice

Puzzle 29 – Beginner

Due to an unfortunate mishap, you've ended up trapped in a medieval dungeon with only three exit doors. Three exit doors sounds pretty good, of course, except that you know what's behind each exit:

Exit One
Behind this door is a crazed lunatic with two very large axes. And he wants your blood.

Exit Two
Waiting to greet you should you choose exit two is a full-on medieval torture chamber, complete with gleeful executioner waiting to try out his 'toys'.

Exit Three
This door contains an enormous lion who hasn't been fed for an entire month. He's known to be extremely vicious.

Now, given this Hobson's choice, which exit door should you pick to give yourself the best chance of survival?

Hobson's Choice

- What is your chance of surviving behind each door?

- I wouldn't bet against the crazed lunatic.

- That executioner will know what he's doing.

- That lion must be really hungry by now, I imagine?

Hobson's Choice

Puzzle 29 – Solutions

Your best bet is to pick exit three, since that lion is surely dead by now if it hasn't eaten for a whole month!

Solving Sequences

Can you work out which letter comes next in each of these real-world sequences?

For example, M T W T F S would be followed by 'S', since the sequence is Monday, Tuesday, Wednesday, Thursday, Friday, Saturday and then 'S' for Sunday.

1

F M A M J J A

2

O T T F F S S

Solving Sequences

Puzzle 30 – Hints

1

- You'll definitely know this sequence. You see it, or parts of it, every single day.

- Perhaps the sequence doesn't start where you normally see it start, but it's perfectly valid to start it at this point too.

2

- You'll definitely know this sequence too – that's absolutely certain.

- Why don't you try counting out the letters, to see if that helps?

Solving Sequences

Puzzle 30 – Solutions

1

The next letter is 'S', since the sequence is the months of the year starting from February, then continuing March, April, May, June, July, August and finally 'S' for September.

2

The next letter is 'E', since the sequence is simply numbers counting up from one, so then continuing two, three, four, five, six, seven and finally 'E' for eight.

Distance Dilemma

Puzzle 31 – Experienced

Today I decide to walk to the supermarket.

I set out from my house, but after walking 500 metres along the road I realize that I have dropped my scarf somewhere along the way, so I turn around and walk back to pick it up. Then I head straight from where my scarf was to the supermarket, which is a distance of 1,000 metres from where my scarf was.

Later on, once I leave the supermarket, I walk straight back to my house without any detours.

My house, the place where I dropped my scarf and the supermarket are all on a completely straight road.

So the question is, how many metres have I walked in total along the road, as described above?

Just to be clear, this is not a trick question – there is a precise numeric solution to be found.

The diagram on the right should help make it clear.

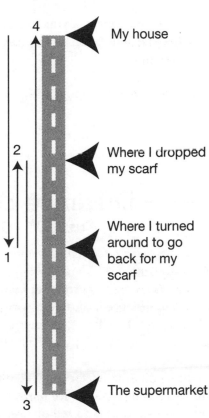

Known distances:
1: 500 metres   3: 1,000 metres
2: Unknown   4: Unknown

Distance Dilemma
Puzzle 31 – Hints

- Try writing it out as a sum. On the way I travel 500 metres, plus some unknown distance shown by arrow '2', and then another 1,000 metres.

- On the way back I travel 1,000 metres minus whatever the length of arrow '2' is, plus another 500 metres.

- So what happens if you add up the distance I travelled on the way and the distance I travelled on the way back?

Distance Dilemma
Puzzle 31 – Solutions

I have walked a total of 3,000 metres along the road.

On the way to the supermarket I walked 500 metres, plus the unknown distance indicated by arrow '2', plus 1,000 metres. On the way back, I walked 1,000 metres *minus* the unknown distance indicated by arrow '2', plus 500 metres.

Therefore the total distance I walked is actually just 500 metres plus 1,000 metres plus 1,000 metres plus 500 metres. The unknown distance is added once and subtracted once, and since adding a value and then subtracting it again gives a net change of zero, I can conclude that the total distance I walked is 3,000 metres.

Join the Dots

Puzzle 32 – Experienced

Here's a challenge that could drive you dotty!

Can you draw a single path that crosses all nine of these dots, without taking your pen off the paper (or leaving the page in any way), and which consists of three perfectly straight lines?

For example, this would be a valid path, although it does not visit all nine dots:

This puzzle *does not* involve tearing or folding the paper, or doing anything other than drawing on this one single page with any tool other than a regular pen or pencil.

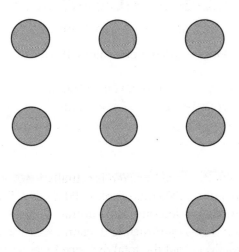

- What's strange about this puzzle?

- Why are the dots so large?

- What does having really large dots make it possible to do, that would not otherwise be possible?

Join the Dots

Puzzle 32 – Solutions

Because the dots are so large, you can draw three diagonal lines at a zig-zag like this:

Lottery Numbers

In a certain national lottery draw, the main prize is split between all those who happen to have a winning ticket for that particular draw.

Players choose six numbers, each in the range 1 to 60, and then six numbers are chosen completely at random to form the winning ticket.

Given this, which of the following strategies is the most sensible:

- Pick numbers which have won *most* often before

- Pick numbers which have won *least* often before

- Pick numbers that are meaningful to you, such as those based on dates

- Pick high numbers that are less likely to be meaningful to either you or other people

- Pick a sequence of continuous numbers

- Pick numbers that are as far apart as possible

- Pick a good mix of odd and even numbers

- Pick either *all* odd or *all* even numbers

Lottery Numbers
Puzzle 33 – Hints

- Are some numbers intrinsically more likely than others?

- How do you think most people choose their numbers?

- Can you influence the result via your selection?

- Who will you have to share your winnings with?

Lottery Numbers
Puzzle 33 – Solutions

The best strategy is to pick numbers that are less likely to have been chosen by others, which means *picking high numbers that are less likely to be meaningful*, such as 57. Lower numbers, that are found in dates, are more frequently chosen because players tend to pick numbers that are meaningful to them in some way. This means that should you win the lottery with low numbers on your ticket then you are far more likely to have to share your winnings with other people, and thus receive less. Single digits are likely to be particularly popular, since people will split higher numbers, for example by splitting 75 into 7 and 5. Picking numbers based on past results will not help, since all future draws are entirely random and have no correlation with previous draws.

Football Focus

1

Two professional football teams walk out onto a football pitch, and yet the referee comes out and blows the final whistle before a single man has kicked a ball.

Despite this, the score is not 0-0 and it is beyond doubt that one team has beaten the other.

How is this possible?

2

At a kids' party the organizer has a large bag with exactly as many footballs in it as there are kids at the party. They don't have any other footballs anywhere else – just the ones in the bag.

Before the kids leave, the organizer gives each one of them a football to keep. Despite this, there is still one football left in the bag.

How is this possible?

1

- It's a regular football match, just as you might see on television.

- Why might no man have kicked a ball? Could someone else?

2

- There are as many footballs as there are kids, and yet still one is left in the bag. Does that sound like a perfectly normal situation, perhaps?

1
It is two women's football teams playing.

2
The last football was left in the bag when it was handed over to the kid.

Escape Artist
Puzzle 35 – Experienced

Imagine that you have a sheet of A4 (or Letter) paper. Better still, go and actually get a sheet of paper of a similar size, and some scissors too.

Now here's the problem. Can you cut the paper in such a way that you can step right through the centre of that piece of paper, without tearing it?

You do actually have to step *through* the paper – in other words, there must be a continuous piece of paper on all sides of you as you step through it.

You also are not allowed to use tape or any other method to reattach the paper to itself once cut. The only tools you are allowed are just that pair of scissors.

This would be easy if you had a really big sheet of paper, so the puzzle is to try and do this using the size specified! You could even do it with a piece of paper the size of this page, but it's slightly easier with A4 (or Letter) paper.

- If you had tape, you could simply cut it into lots of really narrow strips and then tape them together.

- You don't have tape, but can you still do something similar?

- Try folding the paper in half first. Does this give you inspiration?

What you want to do is cut the paper in such a way that it forms a very long single strip of paper. This can be done quite straightforwardly just by folding the paper in half and then cutting through most of its width in alternating directions, then cutting along one edge between the first and last existing cut:

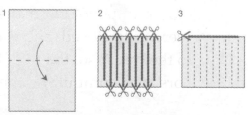

Then just unfold it and step straight through!

1

You're out for a walk in the countryside when you come across the edge of a large forest.

You decide to explore the forest, but you only have a limited amount of time.

What is the maximum distance you can travel into this, or any other, forest?

_____

2

I was out for a stroll when I came across the scene of a crime. A man had been tied to the seat of his car, and a thief had made off with his belongings.

All of the car doors and boot were locked and its windows were fully closed, and there was no damage to the car. Also, the thief hadn't locked the doors after committing the crime.

How is this possible?

Walking Mysteries

1

- There are no numbers in the question, so what kind of answer is likely?

- You're looking for a fraction. What is the maximum distance you can get from any edge of a forest?

2

- Imagine the scene. In what way could the thief have got in?

- What sort of car might it have been?

- Do some cars have other ways of getting in?

Walking Mysteries

1
Halfway. After that, you're starting to get closer to another edge.

2
It was a car with a retractable roof, and the roof was open.

The Sands of Time

Puzzle 37 – Experienced

You have three special sand timers. Each can only be used once – as soon as the timer is turned over and the sand starts to flow, it can never flow back the other way due to a special valve in the centre of the timer.

You have three of these timers, each of which takes a different amount of time for the sand to flow through:

- The first sand timer takes 1 minute to finish

- The second sand timer takes 4 minutes to finish

- The third sand timer takes 7 minutes to finish

You need to measure a total time of exactly **10 minutes**.

How can you do this using just these three sand timers, and without having to guess?

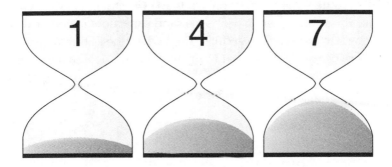

The Sands of Time
Puzzle 37 – Hints

- If you turn the timers over one after another you'll time a total of 12 minutes, which is too long.

- What if you turn them all over together? But if you leave them that way, you'll only time 7 minutes. How can you measure 3 further minutes?

- Is there a way of stopping the timers after you start them?

The Sands of Time
Puzzle 37 – Solutions

Turn over the 1-, 4- and 7-minute timers all at once, then when the 1-minute timer is up, turn over the 4-minute timer. This will pause the 4-minute timer, since the sand can't flow the other way, leaving 3 minutes still to go in it. Then when the 7-minute timer finishes, turn over the 4-minute timer again and let the remaining 3 minutes of sand flow through. The total time elapsed will be 10 minutes.

Runners' Result

Puzzle 38 – Experienced

Jyoti and Sara are taking part in a 100 metres sprint race.

Both of them always run at a constant speed, neither speeding up nor slowing down during the race.

At the end of the race, Jyoti ends up winning by a distance of 10 metres.

'I want a re-run!' demands Sara, so they decide to run the race again. This time they handicap Jyoti by having her start 10 metres back behind the starting line, so she has to run further than Sara.

If both of them run at the same constant speeds that they did for the previous race, who will win?

For a further puzzle, how far back from the finishing line will the loser be when the winner finishes?

Runners' Result

- Jyoti won by 10 metres.

- If she starts 10 metres back, where will she be, relative to Sara, after running 100 metres?

- If they were level after 90 metres for Sara, and 100 metres for Jyoti, who will win the final 10 metres of the race?

Runners' Result

The winner will still be Jyoti, because they will draw level 10 metres from the finish. Jyoti is still running faster, so she will win over the final 10 metres. In fact, she will win by 1 metre.

Square Sculpture
Puzzle 39 – Experienced

Shade some of the squares in this frame to make a picture of your own devising. If you don't know where to start, or are short of inspiration, just begin by filling in some squares at random. You'll probably end up getting inspired at some point!

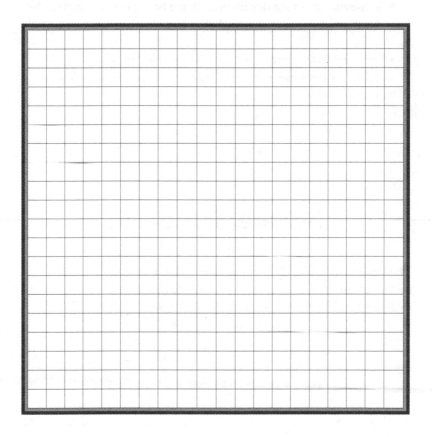

Square Sculpture
Puzzle 39 – Hints

- It's impossible to get this activity 'wrong', since there is no correct answer! You can even use multiple colours if you wish.

- You could create a pattern, perhaps, or just shade some random squares and see what it looks like – you might be surprised!

- Try drawing a monster face – begin with some eyes, then add in the mouth and perhaps nose and any other details you fancy!

- Or you could create a flower of some sort, perhaps? Then add in a bee or the sun or another plant in the background?

Square Sculpture
Puzzle 39 – Solutions

Here are some ideas that might help inspire you!

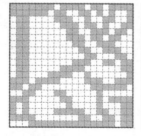  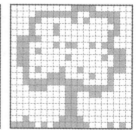

A Cut Above

Roderick has recently moved to a quiet village in a remote part of the country, and is just getting to know a few people around the place.

Having been there for a month, he now needs to get his hair cut.

The village has two barbers, one at each end of the main street, so he needs to decide which one to use.

The barber in the shop next to the village stream always looks incredibly well coiffured, with neatly cut and well-styled hair.

Conversely, the barber in the shop at the other end of the street, next to the village green, has unkempt and unruly hair, without any sense of style.

Which barber should Roderick pick?

- Which one would you go to?

- Who cuts everyone else's hair in the village?

- Who cuts a barber's hair?

A Cut Above

Puzzle 40 – Solutions

Roderick should visit the barber with the shop next to the village green. That barber can't cut his own hair, so with only one other barber in the village it's probably the case that it's the other one making a mess of his hair!

By contrast, the other barber's neat hair is probably being cut by the barber he should choose.

Monthly Matters
Puzzle 41 – Experienced

1

What is it that occurs once in January and once in February, but then doesn't occur again until June, July and August?

_____

2

How many months have twenty-eight days?

_____

3

What occurs once in a year, twice in every month, four times in every week and five times in every weekend?

1

This hint has to be careful not to spell it out ...

2

You definitely won't need a calendar to work this out.

3

Try taking this *very* literally.

Monthly Matters
Puzzle 41 – Solutions

1

The letter 'u'.

2

Every month. The question doesn't say '*only* twenty-eight days'.

3

If you've solved the first question this might have been a bit easier, so long as you paid attention to every 'every'. The answer is the letter 'e'.

Close-up Confusion

Puzzle 42 – Experienced

At first glance, each of the images at the bottom of this page appears to be rather basic. The first is mostly just a squiggly line, and the second is a few circles and a curve. But with a bit of imagination they can become something else.

You can even explain a nearly-empty box:

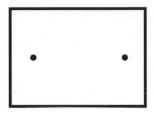

Two polar bears in the snow
(noses visible)

What creative descriptions can you come up with for each of the following images? There is space beneath each one to write a suitable caption.

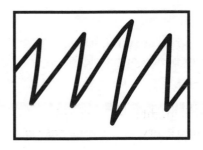

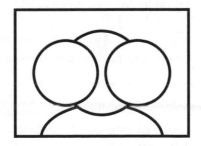

Close-up Confusion

- If you aren't sure where to start, try and think of something each image genuinely looks like, and take it from there.

- For example, the first image could be a close-up of a monster's teeth.

- The second image might be part of a footprint from the underneath of a trainer?

Close-up Confusion

For the first picture, how about some gelled, spiky hair sticking up on top of someone's head?

For the second picture, maybe it's a small creature using binoculars, or a child wearing a giant pair of spectacles?

A Question of Perspective

1

There are 25 people attending a convention for tall people. If each person attending will *only* shake hands with someone that is shorter than them, how many handshakes will take place at the convention?

———————

2

This morning I was 30 years old and yet on my next birthday I will be 32 years old.

How is this possible?

1

- So what possible combinations might you have? A taller person and a shorter person? Two people of the same height?

- Are there any combinations that shake hands and that are permitted?

2

- What might have happened since this morning?

A Question of Perspective
Puzzle 43 – Solutions

1

There will be no handshakes, since people only shake hands with shorter people – and yet for that to happen, the shorter person would have to be breaking the rule.

2

I was born at midday, so I turned 31 at midday today. It is now afternoon and therefore on my next birthday I will turn 32.

It's in the Stars

Puzzle 44 – Experienced

Here's another creative challenge for you, which is a good test of your ability to think about and picture things abstractly:

> Create a picture by joining some or
> all dots using only straight lines.

Lines can only be between the centres of dots, and not between any other point. Despite these restrictions, there's still plenty of opportunity to be creative!

It's in the Stars

Puzzle 44 – Hints

- It can be quite tricky to envisage something that will actually fit the dot pattern, so the best way to tackle this is just to draw some lines and see what you end up with.

- You can use the dots as part of the picture too, especially if you don't join lines to them. For example, perhaps they are stars?

It's in the Stars

Puzzle 44 – Solutions

There's no specific solution here, but here's an attempt to draw a classic arcade-style alien invader. The unused dots here act as background stars!

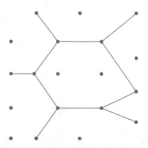

Neighbourly Coins
Puzzle 45 – Experienced

Imagine that you have four coins, as follows:

You can pick up and move the coins as you wish, so feel free to go and get some real coins to try this puzzle out.

The challenge is this:

> Can you arrange the four coins so that each coin
> is simultaneously touching every other coin?

It's possible that this doesn't sound that challenging, but you will probably find it surprisingly tricky when you give it a go! Suffice to say, there *is* a solution!

Neighbourly Coins

- It's easy to make three coins touch each other.

- Stepping up to four is much harder. The best advice is to go and get four real coins and give it a go. It's much harder when you're just looking at the picture.

- Seriously, try thinking outside of the page.

- In fact, try thinking above the page as well.

- Do you need to look at this from a higher level?

Neighbourly Coins

The solution is to make three coins touch by forming a basic triangle shape, and then simply to lay the fourth coin down on top. Easy!

It's impossible if you make the false assumption that the coins must all be on the same level, as the flat picture in the book misleadingly implies!

Timing Issues
Puzzle 46 – Experienced

1

The day before yesterday I was 25 years old, but next year I will be 28 years old.

How can this be true?

2

I live in a city, and yet between the most recent sunset and sunrise I got in and out of bed a staggering 90 times. Despite this, I managed to sleep in excess of 7 hours before every single time that I got up.

Other than by being a great sleeper, how did I manage to achieve this?

1

There's no really sneaky aspect to this – you just need to work out which dates this would be true of.

2

Is there some sort of extreme solution to this? Something that would take you to the ends of the Earth?

Timing Issues
Puzzle 46 – Solutions

1

Today is the 1st of January, and my birthday is on the 31st of December. So if the day before yesterday I was 25, today I am 26. At the end of this year I will turn 27, and then at the end of next year I will turn 28.

2

I'm living in Reykjavik in Iceland, where the sun never sets during the summer months. Other extreme northern cities are also possible.

Cats and Dogs

Puzzle 47 – Experienced

A household contains three cats and three dogs, and they all need to be taken to a veterinary practice for their injections.

Only two animals can fit in their owner's car to travel to the veterinary practice, so the owner needs to work out a suitable way of transferring them all.

The problem the owner has is that she cannot ever have more of her dogs than her cats in any place, either at home or at the veterinary practice, or otherwise the dogs will attack the cats. In other words, there must always be at least as many cats as there are dogs either at home or at the practice.

Also, the owner cannot bear to be without at least one of her animals, so every time she drives in her car she must always have at least one animal with her.

She also can never leave an animal alone in the car, so when she arrives home or at the veterinary practice all of the animals must get out and join any others that are already there. Even when accompanied by the owner there must never be more dogs than cats in either place, not even just for a moment before returning back in the car.

Without dropping any animals off anywhere else, how can she safely transfer all of her animals to the practice using just her one vehicle?

Cats and Dogs

- There is a logical way to do this – it's just a question of finding a suitable sequence of journeys.

- Remember that animals always get out and that dogs can never outnumber cats, so you can't, for example, transfer a dog and a cat to a place that already has a dog, even if you immediately return with the dog. This rule prevents you from solving the puzzle trivially by simply driving back and forth with a dog in the car the entire time.

- Start by transferring a cat and a dog to the practice. Now you must come back with an animal since the vehicle can never be empty – which one will it be?

Cats and Dogs
Puzzle 47 – Solutions

The solution requires 11 steps, although there is more than one way of doing it. Here's one method, representing animal counts in the form home/practice, and abbreviating cat to 'c' and dog to 'd'.

Start = 3c3d/none; drive 1c1d to vet = 2c2d/1c1d;
drive 1c to home = 3c2d/1d; drive 2d to vet = 3c/3d;
drive 1d to home = 3c1d/2d; drive 2c to vet = 1c1d/2c2d;
drive 1c1d to home = 2c2d/1c1d; drive 2c to vet = 2d/3c1d;
drive 1d to home = 3d/3c; drive 2d to vet = 1d/3c2d;
drive 1d to home = 2d/3c1d; drive 2d to vet = none/3c3d. Done!

The tricky step here is driving *two* animals home at one point!

Darkening Deduction
Puzzle 48 – Experienced

Black out some of the words, or even part-words, in this extract from *The Adventures of Sherlock Holmes*, so what's left forms a very short story of your own invention.

I had seen little of Holmes lately. My marriage had drifted us away from each other. My own complete happiness, and the home-centred interests which rise up around the man who first finds himself master of his own establishment, were sufficient to absorb all my attention, while Holmes, who loathed every form of society with his whole Bohemian soul, remained in our lodgings in Baker Street, buried among his old books. He was still, as ever, deeply attracted by the study of crime, and occupied his immense faculties and extraordinary powers of observation in following out those clues, and clearing up those mysteries which had been abandoned as hopeless by the official police. From time to time I heard some vague account of his doings: of his summons to Odessa in the case of the Trepoff murder, of his clearing up of the singular tragedy of the Atkinson brothers at Trincomalee, and finally of the mission which he had accomplished so delicately and successfully for the reigning family of Holland. Beyond these signs of his activity, however, which I merely shared with all the readers of the daily press, I knew little of my former friend and companion.

One night—it was on the twentieth of March, 1888—I was returning from a journey to a patient (for I had now returned to civil practice), when my way led me through Baker Street. As I passed the well-remembered door, which must always be associated in my mind with my wooing, and with the dark incidents of the Study in Scarlet, I was seized with a keen desire to see Holmes again, and to know how he was employing his extraordinary powers. His rooms were brilliantly lit, and, even as I looked up, I saw his tall, spare figure pass twice in a dark silhouette against the blind. He was pacing the room swiftly, eagerly, with his head sunk upon his chest and his hands clasped behind him. To me, who knew his every mood and habit, his attitude and manner told their own story. He was at work again.

Darkening Deduction
Puzzle 48 – Hints

Not sure how to start? Just pick some words to cross out or leave in, and see where you end up! Here's an example, just to show how it works:

I had seen little of ~~Holmes lately. My~~ marriage ~~had drifted us away from each other. My own complete~~ happiness, ~~and~~ the ~~home-centred interests which rise up around the~~ man who ~~first~~ finds himself master of his own ~~establishment, were sufficient to absorb all my~~ attention, ~~while Holmes, who loathed every form of society with~~ his whole ~~Bohemian soul, remained in our lodgings in Baker Street,~~ buried among his ~~old books. He was still, as ever,~~ deeply ~~attracted by the study of crime, and occupied his~~ immense faculties ~~and extraordinary powers of observation in following out those clues,~~ and ~~clearing up those mysteries which had been~~ abandoned as hopeless ~~by the official police. From time to time~~ I heard ~~some vague account of his doings: of his~~ summons to ~~Odessa in the case of the Trepoff murder, of his clearing up of the singular~~ tragedy ~~of the Atkinson brothers at Trincomalee,~~ and ~~finally of the mission which he had~~ accomplish~~ed so delicately and successfully for the reigning family of Holland. Beyond~~ these signs ~~of his activity, however, which I merely shared~~ with ~~all the readers of the daily press, I knew little of~~ my former friend ~~and companion.~~

One ~~night—it was on the twentieth of~~ March~~, 1888—~~ I was ~~returning from a journey to a patient (for I had now returned to civil practice), when my way~~ led ~~me~~ through ~~Baker Street. As I passed the well-remembered door, which must always be associated in~~ my mind with ~~my~~ wooing, and ~~with the dark incidents of the Study in Scarlet,~~ I was seized with a keen desire to see ~~Holmes again, and to know how he was employing his~~ extraordinary powers~~. His rooms were brilliantly lit, and, even as I looked up, I saw his tall, spare figure pass twice~~ in a dark ~~silhouette against the blind. He was pacing the~~ room ~~swiftly, eagerly, with his head sunk upon his chest and his hands clasped behind him. To me, who knew his every mood and habit, his attitude and manner told their own story. He was~~ at work ~~again.~~

1

Can you name something that will always taste better than it sounds?

2

Dave tells me that his friend predicts the future, and what's more Dave is not lying. How can this possibly be true?

1

It's something you take with you everywhere you go.

2

If Dave's telling the truth, what *precisely* does that mean?

1

Your tongue!

2

Dave is telling the truth – his friend *does* predict the future. Just not very well. Dave is accurate; his friend may not be.

Number Nonsense

1

Nobody would disagree that one comes before two, but in what circumstances would an intelligent person agree that two comes after three, and that three comes after four?

2

Imagine that you have just picked up a tennis ball, or any other perfectly spherical object, and have marked three points on it completely at random.

What is the chance that all three points have ended up on the same half of the ball?

1

Is there any situation in which this might be true? It clearly isn't true when they're in normal numerical order.

2

Think about it – there's no catch here. Really do imagine doing it, or if you wish then get a ball and try it out!

Number Nonsense
Puzzle 50 – Solutions

1

This will be true in a dictionary, when the numbers are sorted in alphabetical order.

2

It's a certainty. There will always be a way to divide the ball in half such that the three points are all in the same half, or at the very least are all on the boundary of that half.

If you have trouble visualizing this, imagine a flat version of a sphere, or in other words a circle. Any two points in this circle must be in the same half, or at least on the boundary of some half.

Square Dance

Here's another 'matchstick' puzzle.

This problem seems difficult at first glance, but there is a perfectly sensible solution to be found!

Start by arranging twelve matchsticks (or pencils, or straws, or any narrow and long objects) as follows:

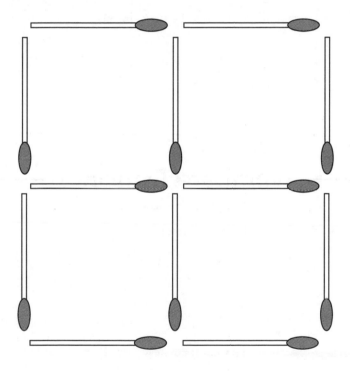

Now, by removing just two matches, can you change the picture so there are exactly two squares – no more, no less. All matches must form part of the squares – there can't be any leftover 'sticking-out' matches.

Puzzle 51 – Hints

- It's quite fun to solve this by experimenting with real matches, or pencils or straws or what have you.

- It would be easy to remove, for example, the two vertical straws on the right-hand side to leave two squares, but this wouldn't be valid because you'd be leaving some 'sticking-out' matches.

- Do the squares all need to be the same size?

Square Dance

Puzzle 51 – Solutions

The solution is to make two squares of different sizes:

Casual Acquaintance

The other day I was on a visit to the town where I grew up, which I hadn't been to for many years.

While I was there, I ran into an old school friend who I hadn't seen for a long time. After reminiscing about 'the old days' for some time, we started to talk about our current lives.

My friend had always spoken in riddles, and this time was no different. They said,

> 'I married someone you've never met and don't know, and this child I'm with is our son.'

The son said hello to me, and so I asked him what his name was. He replied,

> 'It's the same as my mother's.'

To which I replied,

> 'Oh, so your name is Jordan!'

But how did I know the child's name?

Casual Acquaintance

- Have I met the mother before?

- Would I have met them when I was at school, perhaps?

- In what circumstance could I know their name?

Casual Acquaintance

The person you're speaking to is Jordan, who is the mother in question, so of course you know her name!

Rhymes, not Crimes

Not everyone is a poet, but you can surely think of at least one word that rhymes with almost any other word.

Now take that innate ability to the next level, by writing just one line to form a complete two-line poem. Whoever said that poems needed to be long?

For example, given the line:
Each morning I awake with glee,
... you could perhaps follow it with the rhyming line:
Yearning for a cup of tea.

See what you can come up with for each of these examples:

1.
When the fairground comes to town,

_____

2.
The earliest dream I ever had,

_____

- Start by thinking of some words that rhyme with the last word of the given line.

- Do any of these words seem to fit in any way with the first line?

- It doesn't matter if the connection is ridiculous – this often makes it funnier, which is usually a good thing when it comes to two-line poems!

Rhymes, not Crimes
Puzzle 53 – Solutions

Here are two possible endings, both of which are particularly dull! See if you can come up with something more exciting!

1.
When the fairground comes to town,
I grab my change and dash on down.

2.
The earliest dream I ever had,
Was when I was a little lad.

Pouring More

Due to some rather poor party planning, you have turned up to cater a children's party without the exact amounts of lemonade that you promised.

The host, who is particularly fussy about having precise quantities, requires two separate containers, each containing exactly four litres of lemonade. All you have, however, are three containers that you know hold exactly three, five and eight litres respectively.

The three- and five-litre containers are empty, but the eight-litre container is full. You also have a funnel, which allows you to pour liquid between containers without spilling any.

How can you measure out two containers, each with *precisely* four litres of lemonade? There is an exact solution to find – doing it 'by eye' is not the solution!

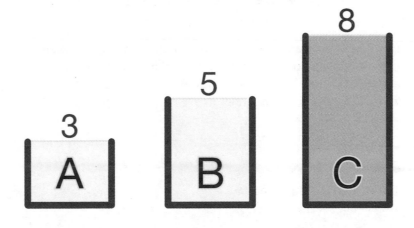

Pouring More

- If you already tried the wine puzzle earlier in the book, you'll have a head start on this version.

- The secret is to progressively try and form different quantities of lemonade, and to use these to form further new different quantities.

- Start by pouring C into B, giving 0-5-3.

- Next pour B into A to give 3-2-3.

- Now you can form a new amount of 6 litres by pouring A into C.

Pouring More

This takes two more steps than the earlier puzzle with 2, 5 and 7 litre containers. Pour C into B for 0-5-3; B into A for 3-2-3; A into C for 0-2-6; B into A for 2-0-6; C into B for 2-5-1; B into A for 3-4-1; A into C for 0-4-4. You're done!

1

If I weren't there, you wouldn't be,
Although you often curse at me.
Sometimes I cry and have a fall;
Then my tears soak it all.
So I leave and go to sea.
What am I?

2

I walk in file, a loyal troop,
My life lived in a group.
I serve my family, and my queen,
Always keeping to routine.
To see me you must stoop.
What am I?

1

- What do you often curse at and yet without it you wouldn't exist ('be')?

- What can 'cry' and go to sea?

2

- What might walk in file?

- What serves a queen?

- What size is something that you need to stoop to see?

Puzzling Personifications
Puzzle 55 – Solutions

1

The rain fulfils all of these descriptions: you (or the world in general at any case) need it, yet often curse it. It sometimes falls. Like crying, it soaks everything, and then ultimately it drains away to the sea.

2

An ant fits this description. It walks in file and lives its life in service to its queen. It is too small to see clearly without stooping, and lives in a group that follows routine behaviours.

Square Obstruction

Look at this empty square. There's something concealed behind it, but what do you think it is?

Given just the parts that are sticking out from behind the square, what do you think is actually *behind* that square?

Grab a pencil, and draw in what you think it might be!

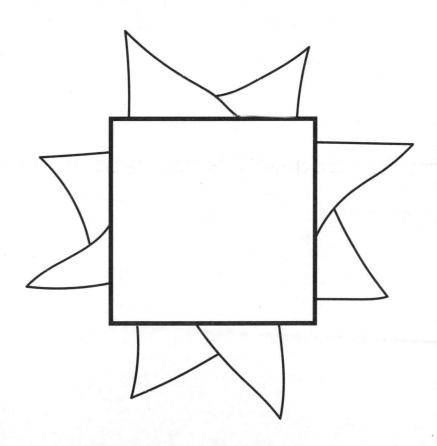

Square Obstruction
Puzzle 56 – Hints

- Is it some kind of origami experiment?

- Perhaps it's eight small yachts all lying in a stack?

- Maybe you can see a windmill on a beach?

Square Obstruction
Puzzle 56 – Solutions

There's no correct solution, but how about this flower?

The Truth Will Out

Puzzle 57 – Experienced

Six people are standing in a room, and each speaks to you in turn.

They conclude their speeches by saying the following things to you, one per person as indicated:

- **Person A**: Exactly one person is lying

- **Person B**: Exactly two people are lying

- **Person C**: Exactly three people are lying

- **Person D**: Exactly four people are lying

- **Person E**: Exactly five people are lying

- **Person F**: All of us are lying

Which of these people, A to F, if any at all, have told you the truth?

The Truth Will Out

- If A was telling the truth, then five people would be telling the truth. But those five statements would all contradict each other, so A can't be telling the truth.

- If F was telling the truth, then their statement 'All of us are lying' couldn't be true, so F can't be telling the truth.

- So what can you conclude?

The Truth Will Out

Persons A to D must all be lying, because in each case there would need to be at least two people telling the truth, but no two people say the same thing and they all contradict each other.

Person F must be lying, because if they were telling the truth then they'd be contradicting themself.

That leaves person E. Person E can't be lying because if they were then either they would all be lying, which would mean person F is telling the truth – and we know that isn't possible – or one of A to D would be telling the truth – also not possible.

So E is telling the truth, and everyone else is lying.

Secondary Sequences

Puzzle 58 – Experienced

Can you work out which letter comes next in each of these real-world sequences?

For example, M T W T F S would be followed by 'S', since the sequence is Monday, Tuesday, Wednesday, Thursday, Friday, Saturday and then 'S' for Sunday.

1

N U S J M E V

<hr>

2

F S T F F S S

Secondary Sequences

1

- You'll know this sequence, but it's possible you might not quite be sure of the precise order. However, there are only eight things in this set so you can use process of elimination to be sure of your answer once you realize what the sequence is!

- You normally see this out-of-the-world sequence in the opposite order.

2

- This sequence is related to one you've seen earlier in this book. It has something to do with numbers.

Secondary Sequences

1

The next letter is 'M', since the sequence is the planets of the solar system moving inwards, so starting from Neptune, then Uranus, Saturn, Jupiter, Mars, Earth, Venus and finally 'M' for Mercury.

2

The next letter is 'E', since the sequence is ordinal numbers counting up from first, then continuing second, third, fourth, fifth, sixth, seventh and finally 'E' for eighth.

Square Cut
Puzzle 59 – Experienced

For this challenge you'll need a square of paper and a pair of scissors. A small sheet from a memo block is ideal, or otherwise you can simply cut a rectangular sheet of paper into a rough square. You don't need a large sheet of paper – in fact, pretty much any size will do.

The challenge is to reproduce a pattern *only* by repeatedly folding the paper in half, and then making a *single* straight line cut.

You can fold either diagonally or horizontally/vertically, just so long as the paper ends up being exactly half the size after the fold that it was before. The single cut, which is the final step, can be wherever you like, then unfold the paper. For example, you can form a rotated square in the centre of a piece of paper like this:

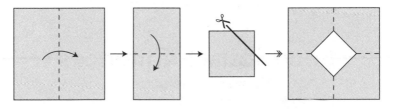

Now work out how to form this result by following these rules:

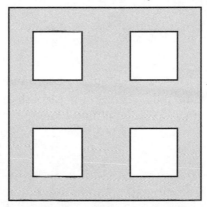

Square Cut
Puzzle 59 – Hints

- There are four separate cuts, so you must fold it at least twice.

- In fact, to form square cut-outs you must have to fold it at least three times, because after just two folds you'd need two cuts to make four squares.

- Start by folding vertically in half.

- Then fold horizontally in half.

- Now fold twice more, and then cut.

Square Cut
Puzzle 59 – Solutions

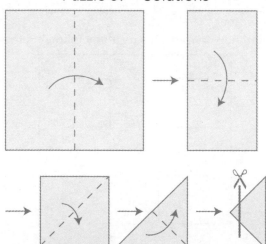

A Simple Question

You are meeting up with two old friends, both of whom say they have brought a present for you.

You all enjoy setting challenges for each other, so the friends have decided to make things interesting. They tell you that one of them has brought a great present that you are sure to enjoy, while the other has brought some smelly old socks with holes in that are of no use to anyone. To make it much harder for you to tell which is which, each present has been wrapped in an almost identical box, so only the two friends know which box is which.

The challenge they set you is this:

> You can only ask one question, and you
> can only ask it of one of us.

> One of us will definitely answer the question truthfully,
> and the other one of us will definitely lie.

What question should you ask, so as to be sure of getting the great present rather than the smelly old socks?

A Simple Question
Puzzle 60 – Hints

- You have no way of knowing which one is the liar and which one tells the truth, so your question will need to work no matter which the person you ask turns out to be.

- Indeed, you won't know if they have lied or told the truth, so the question needs to give the same answer no matter which is the case!

- So what question can you ask that will work in this circumstance?

- Can you involve both of them in a single question, even though just one of them can answer it?

A Simple Question
Puzzle 60 – Solutions

You should ask which box the *other* person would tell you to open, if you wanted the great present. Then pick the other box to whatever they say to actually open.

This works because if you happen to choose the person who tells the truth, he will tell you the wrong box since he will be telling you what the liar would say. If, conversely, you happen to choose the person who always lies, he will tell you the opposite of what the person who tells the truth would say, which will of course also be the wrong box.

Either way, they will recommend the wrong box and by opening the other one you will be guaranteed the present you wanted.

A Knotty Issue

Imagine that you have a piece of string of around fifty centimetres length or more in your hands, or better still go and get a piece of string if you have one and place it down on a table in front of you. It should be laid in one long line, and not overlapping itself or tied in any way.

Now face the table, or imagine facing the table if you don't have any string. Next, pick up one end of the string between the thumb and forefinger of the left hand, and then pick up the other end of the string between the thumb and forefinger of the right hand. You should now be holding one end of the string in one hand, and the other end in the other hand.

All you have to do now is tie a knot in the string, but there is one very important condition:

> You cannot let go of the string
> with either hand at any point.

Once you have successfully tied the knot you can then let go, and the knot must survive both ends of the string being pulled hard apart from each other – in other words, it must be a proper knot!

There's no catch in the wording here – there is a way of doing this genuinely without letting go at all, and it does not require any manipulation of the string prior to picking it up. It certainly doesn't involve yanking the string about randomly and hoping it accidentally forms a knot!

A Knotty Issue

- You really should give this a go with actual string if you can. In the absence of string you could use an electrical cable – but if so then don't pull any knot you manage to form too tight so as to avoid damage to the cable!

- Short of bits of cable catching on each other by chance, you'll have a hard time tying a knot without letting go!

- Given the question is clear that you can't cheat in any way once you've picked up the string, and you can't pre-fold the string, what is there that you *can* do to make this possible?

A Knotty Issue

The secret is to fold your arms before you pick up the string. When you fold them, you must make sure that one hand is on top of the other arm, and the other hand is sitting under the remaining arm. If you don't, this won't work. Now if you unfold your arms, you'll find the string magically knotted – this is actually a great party trick!

If your string is short then this can make it hard to pick up both ends simultaneously, which is why the question is worded to allow you to pick up the two ends separately.

A Likely Story

1

You have a drawer full of loose ribbons, all identical in design but varying only in colour. Given that you have six red ribbons, eight blue ribbons and ten green ribbons, how many ribbons do you have to take out of the drawer to be sure of having at least three ribbons of the same colour? Assume that you are drawing them at random, not looking into the drawer and simply picking those of the same colour!

———

2

At a party, eight different children are each given a different toy car, which they then leave lying around on the floor. A parent at the party doesn't know which car belongs to which child, so he picks them up and then gives one at random to each child. What is the likelihood that exactly seven of the children end up with the correct car?

1

- Think it through in your head, or work it out on a piece of paper. Imagine that the first one you draw is red. And the second is a different colour. And then the third is different too.

- Which ribbons can possibly come next, in the worst-possible case where you need to draw as many as possible?

2

- What would the eighth child end up with?

- There are no mathematical calculations required.

A Likely Story
Puzzle 62 – Solutions

1

Seven ribbons. In the worst-case scenario you draw two red, two green and two blue for the first six ribbons. At this point the seventh ribbon is guaranteed to be the third of a colour.

2

No chance at all. With only one child left, if the others all have the correct car then he or she must do too, so you couldn't have *exactly* seven right. You either have to have one to six or instead all eight correct.

Shading Skills
Puzzle 63 – Expert

Shade some of the squares in this frame to make a picture of your own devising. You can use colour if you wish, but just a regular pencil is perfectly good – there are some ideas overleaf if you feel short of inspiration, but why not just shade some squares at random and see what happens?

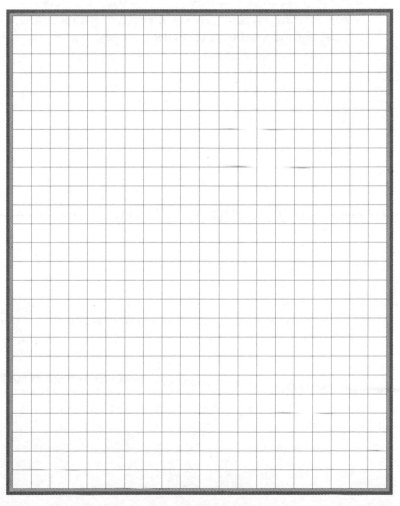

Shading Skills

- You can't go wrong on this one, so just pick a square and shade it. Then pick another, and so on – the chances are you'll end up seeing that it looks a bit like something you recognize, or you can expand it into a pattern of some type.

- It doesn't have to be a picture, or even a pattern. It could be some writing – drawing text with a limited number of squares like this can be quite challenging, and lead to some interesting stylized designs.

Shading Skills
Puzzle 63 – Solutions

Here are some ideas that might help inspire you!

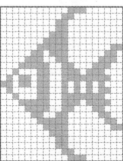
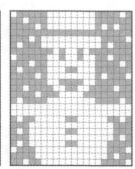

An Extra Cut

Imagine that you have a square of paper and have cut it up into the pieces shown here:

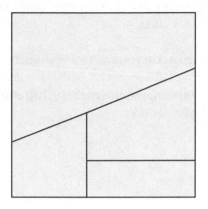

Or, better still, take an actual square of paper and cut it up as shown.

Now rearrange the pieces into this alternative layout:

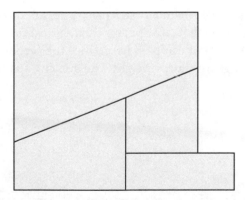

Can you explain where the extra piece of the square comes from?

An Extra Cut

- Is all as it seems?

- Try actually getting a square of paper and cutting it up as shown in the top picture.

- Now rearrange it. Do you notice anything?

- What if you rearrange it on top of the original image?

An Extra Cut

In puzzles like this, where an extra piece appears on rearranging, it's always the case that two apparently identical outlines are in fact different. The same applies here, since the second 'square' is in fact a rectangle of shorter height. The missing space is shown here:

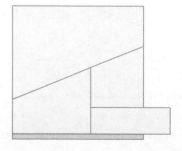

Door Decision
Puzzle 65 – Expert

You're visiting the fairground and are trying to win a toy animal at a stall.

The stall features a game of complete chance, where you must choose one of three doors to open. You know that behind one of the doors is the animal you want to win, whereas the other doors both have nothing behind. Therefore you have a one in three chance of immediately picking the right door, since you have no reason to favour one over another. Only the stallholder knows behind which of the doors he has hidden the animal.

You pick a door, but rather than open it immediately the stallholder opens one of the other two doors, that you didn't choose, and shows you that there is no animal behind it.

He then offers you a choice:

> 'Do you want to switch to the other
> unopened door, or do you want to stick
> with your original choice of door?'

So what should you do? Should you switch doors? And does it matter? What is the likelihood of winning for the door you originally chose, and what is the likelihood of winning if you switch doors?

Door Decision

- There are two doors left, so is it just a one in two chance which door the animal is behind?

- If you came up to the game with just two doors to choose from, it would indeed be a 50:50 choice between the two doors. But that's not the situation – the stall holder has already eliminated one of the original *three* options.

- You had a 1 in 3 chance when you picked the door originally, and you know that the store holder has deliberately picked the one of the other two doors that he knew *didn't* have the animal behind, so what does this tell you?

Door Decision

Puzzle 65 – Solutions

You should definitely switch doors. It's tempting to think it doesn't matter, but the stallholder has actually given you information you didn't have when you made your original guess – which you already know had a 1 in 3 chance of being right. He has deliberately picked the one of the two remaining doors that has no prize, so this doesn't make your original choice more likely to be correct – it remains at its original 1 in 3 chance.

Essentially the stallholder has now changed the three options into just two options: your *one* original door, or the *two* other doors of which he has already opened one. So swap and your chances of winning become 2 in 3. Therefore you will be twice as likely to win!

Dotty Dilemma
Puzzle 66 – Expert

Here's another dot-joining dilemma, but this time you can't use either of the tricks used on the previous occasions!

Can you draw a single path that joins all nine of these dots, without taking your pen off the paper (or leaving the page in any way), and which consists of four perfectly straight lines?

For example, this would be a valid path, although it does not visit all nine dots:

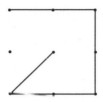

This puzzle *does not* involve tearing or folding the paper, or doing anything other than drawing on this one single page with any tool other than a regular pen or pencil.

Dotty Dilemma

Puzzle 66 – Hints

- You can't use the tricks from previous dot-joining puzzles, but on the face of it this doesn't seem to be possible. So clearly you need to think outside the box!

- No, seriously – try thinking outside the box ...

- What if some of the lines were to journey outside the perimeter of the dots?

Dotty Dilemma

Puzzle 66 – Solutions

The secret to solving this puzzle is to extend the lines that you draw outside the boundary of the dots. Once you do this, it becomes relatively simple to solve. For example:

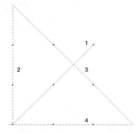

Note that this will involve drawing over some of the text, but that's not forbidden by the rules!

An Explosive Enigma
Puzzle 67 – Expert

A troop of soldiers are on a march across the countryside, and as part of their training they are carrying small explosive devices that are set to detonate if dropped or thrown onto a hard surface.

In the training version of the device the actual explosion will be completely harmless, but each soldier wants to avoid the device detonating in order to not have to do a further march on a later date.

Halfway through the march the soldiers pass along a hard path that leads across the face of a tall cliff. To one side is a solid rock face, while to the other is a long plummet to rocky ground below.

It's at this point that the soldiers are instructed to halt, and one by one they must drop their explosive devices over the edge of the cliff. They don't throw them, but simply hold both arms together, holding the device in both hands, and then open their hands and let them go.

Despite each soldier in turn following this order, none of the explosive devices go off. They are not faulty, and the soldiers do not help each other in any way. Neither are they simply all lucky.

The soldiers have not been allowed to modify the devices in any way, and nor are they allowed to place anything on top of the rock below to soften the impact. It's also not windy, so it is not the case that the devices are being blown onto a softer landing area.

Why did none of the devices detonate?

- The soldiers each did something to stop their device from detonating, but it didn't involve altering the device.

- If they can't do anything before they let go, what can they do *after* they've let go?

The soldiers let go of the devices but then simply swung their arms around beneath and caught them quickly again before they fell very far, slowing their descent with their hands. If you try this with a suitable object yourself (preferably neither explosive nor easily breakable!) you'll find it's actually very easy to do, so that's how they all succeeded in doing this.

Childish Behaviour

Two children have gone exploring, and are thrilled to have come across a cave hidden behind some foliage on a nearby hillside.

Ignoring their parents' clear instructions not to do anything foolish, they head on into the cave without a further thought.

It's dark in the cave, and neither child has a torch, so they can't see where they're going. One child goes much further ahead than the other, disturbing a pile of coal dust in what must originally have been an open-drift mine.

Startled by the sudden disturbance, both children rush out of the cave, screaming with a mix of both fear and delight.

When they reach the open air they both run straight back to their respective homes.

The child who disturbed the coal dust has a dirty face, but when he gets home he makes no effort to wash. The other child has a perfectly clean face, yet by contrast as soon as he gets home he rushes to the sink and scrubs his face.

Assuming that neither child would ordinarily wash their face when they got home, and that this isn't down to just pure chance, what reasonable explanation can there be for this strange behaviour?

- This is easier if you picture the scene.

- Imagine that you're the child with the dirty face. What have you actually seen?

- Imagine that you're the other child. What differs about your perception of events, compared to the other child?

Childish Behaviour
Puzzle 68 – Solutions

The child with the clean face has seen the child with the dirty face when he left the cave, so when he got home the first thing he did was wash what he assumed was his own dirty face.

Conversely, the child with the dirty face has seen the child with the clean face when he left the cave, so because it was dark inside the cave he has not realized that his own face is covered in dirty coal dust. Therefore he didn't think to go and wash when he got home.

Flowering of the Imagination

Here's another creative challenge for you, which is a good test of your ability to think about and picture things abstractly:

Create a picture by joining some or
all dots using only straight lines.

Lines can only be between the centres of dots, and not between any other point. Despite these restrictions, there's still plenty of opportunity to be creative!

149

- It's quite tricky to envisage something that will actually fit the dot pattern, so the best way to tackle this is just to draw some lines and see what you end up with.

- You can use the dots as part of the picture too, especially if you don't join lines to them.

- You could rotate the book if you'd rather view your dots or picture from a different angle.

Flowering of the Imagination
Puzzle 69 – Solutions

There's no specific solution to this challenge, but here's one idea. This is intended to look like two flowers, although with a bit of adjustment it could also have been a picture of two kites!

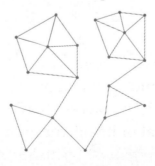

A Cubic Conundrum

1

Samantha has been working hard all day at building a large, cube-shaped piece of furniture that she bought at the local furniture store.

When she's done, she sits back and admires her handiwork. She is able to examine all six sides of the cuboid just by moving her head, and without moving any other part of her body.

Given that there are no mirrors or anything else reflective anywhere near, how is it that she is able to do this?

2

Can you work out a way to cut a cube of cheese into six equal pieces using just three cuts? The pieces should either all be identical or be mirror images of one another. There must be no leftover pieces.

1

- Where might you get that view from?

2

- You need to think three-dimensionally here. If you have an actual block of hard cheese handy, you could always try out your ideas in practice! It's a potentially tasty method, too.

- How would you divide it into two equal parts? Is there some way you can cut it where you would make a similar type of cut three times and result in six parts?

- It's easier to end up with *eight* identical parts, but the question forbirds you from throwing anything away!

A Cubic Conundrum
Puzzle 70 – Solutions

1

She's sitting inside the furniture cube, so can easily see all sides.

2

Place a knife flat along one top edge, then cut straight through to the diagonally opposite bottom edge. Then move the knife to a neighbouring top edge and cut again to the diagonally opposite edge. Then cut diagonally through the centre of the top face straight down to the bottom face. You'll end up with six pieces that are all the same or are mirror images of each other. The three cuts look like this:

1

A woman is lying dead in a wheat field with an unopened package beside her. None of the wheat around her has been trampled and so it is not clear how she got there.

Can you explain what led to this situation?

2

A man marries over one hundred different women and yet he hasn't had to divorce any of them, and they are all perfectly happy.

Given that the man is not polygamous, how is this possible?

1

- Why isn't the wheat trampled at all? How did she get there?

- What might the package be?

2

- How has he managed to marry so many people?

- It's almost as if it's his job!

1

The person was a parachutist, and her parachute – the package lying alongside her – failed to open. She fell straight into the middle of the field, avoiding crushing any of the wheat around her.

2

The man has married each of the women to other men – he is a priest, or a registrar.

Here's another matchstick puzzle.

This problem seems difficult at first glance, but there is a perfectly sensible solution to be found!

Start by arranging eight matchsticks (or pencils, or straws, or any narrow and long objects) as follows:

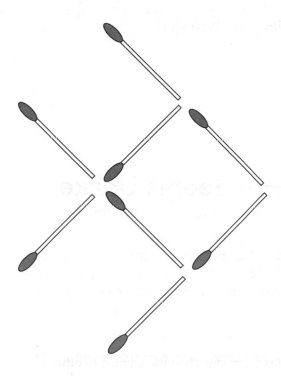

Now, by moving exactly three matches, can you change the picture so that the fish is facing in the opposite direction? The relative arrangement of matches must remain the same – but the fish must now point to the left, rather than the right.

Fishy Facing

- It's quite fun to solve this by experimenting with real matches, or pencils or straws or what have you.

- If you could move an extra match, this wouldn't be so hard. Is there some slight trick to this?

- You know the fish has to face the opposite direction, but does it have to be at the same vertical position on the page?

Fishy Facing

The solution is to move the fish down (or up) the page while reversing it, which reduces the number of matches that need to be moved to three:

Thirsty Work

Puzzle 73 – Expert

I have a bottle of cola, and I want to drink as much of it as I can.

I've promised, however, to leave exactly half the bottle for my friend, but I don't appear to have any accurate way of measuring this. The bottle is narrower at the top and indented at the bottom and middle, so I can't just assume that half way down the bottle is half of the cola.

Without having to guess, and without requiring any tools other than just the bottle itself, how can I be sure to leave my friend almost exactly half a bottle of cola?

To be clear, there is a way to measure the liquid almost precisely, using just the bottle – it doesn't have or require any labels or marks on it of any sort, and it doesn't involve any modifications to the bottle.

- If the bottle was a perfect cylinder, how would you measure it?

- Is there any way to create a similar measuring situation with a plastic bottle that contains dimples and a narrow neck?

- Try looking at things from a different angle.

Thirsty Work

Puzzle 73 – Solutions

Simply put the bottle down flat on its side. Now it is easy to see if there is more or less than half of the bottle left, since halfway up will in fact be *exactly* half the volume of the bottle.

Connecting Coins
Puzzle 74 – Expert

Imagine that you have five coins, as follows:

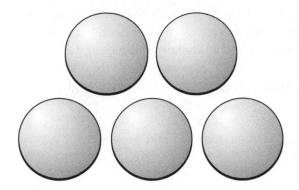

You can pick up and move the coins as you wish, so feel free to go and get some real coins to try this puzzle out.

The challenge is this:

> Can you arrange the five coins so that each coin is simultaneously touching every other coin?

If you haven't yet tried the four-coin version (see puzzle 45 on page 101), it's probably best to go back and try that first.

Just like for that puzzle, there's also a solution to this one!

Connecting Coins

- It's easy to make three coins touch each other.

- Stepping up to four is much harder, so as the text says you should turn to page 101 if you haven't yet tried that puzzle.

- For five coins you're going to have think 'out of the page', as you did for the four-coin version.

- You're going to have to think *really* out of the page. In fact, you're going to have to build some kind of structure with the coins.

Connecting Coins

The solution is to put down a coin, and lay two on top of it. They may slope slightly away from the centre, but that doesn't matter. Next, hold the other two coins on top to form a standing-up triangle profile. Their bases should be resting either on or alongside the bottom coin, and they will be leaning against the two coins on the second layer in the process. That's it!

The left-hand picture shows the layout clearly, but the practical solution will look more like the picture on the right-hand side.

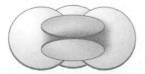 

A Matter of Timing
Puzzle 75 – Expert

I have two regular sand timers, each of which takes a different amount of time for the sand to flow through:

- The first sand timer takes 5 minutes for the sand to flow through

- The second sand timer takes 7 minutes for the sand to flow through

Using these two timers, and nothing else, how can I measure the passage of exactly **9 minutes** of time?

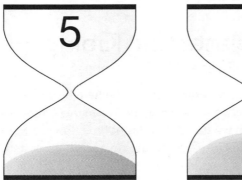

- If I run one after the other I'll count 12 minutes, which is too long.

- If I turn them over together and leave them be then that will only measure 7 minutes.

- So what can I do to change that?

Turn over both timers together, and then when the 5 minute one finishes turn it straight back over again. When the 7 minute one then finishes you'll have had 2 minutes of time flow through the 5 minute one. This leaves 3 minutes to go, but if you now immediately turn this back over again then those 2 minutes of time will flow the other way. When that is also complete then a total of 9 minutes will have elapsed.

You, Poet

Not everyone is a poet, but you can surely think of at least one word that rhymes with almost any other word.

Now take that innate ability to the next level, by writing just one line to form a complete two-line poem. Whoever said that poems needed to be long?

For example, given the line:
Each morning I awake with glee,
... you could perhaps follow it with the rhyming line:
Yearning for a cup of tea.

See what you can come up with for each of these examples:

1.
I like to sit at night and relax,

_____

2.
The most wondrous thing just happened today,

_____

You, Poet

- Start by thinking of some words that rhyme with the last word of the given line.

- Do any of these words seem to fit in any way with the first line?

- It doesn't matter if the connection is ridiculous – this often makes it funnier, which is usually a good thing when it comes to two-line poems!

You, Poet

Here are two possible endings, both of which are particularly dull! See if you can come up with something more exciting!

1.
I like to sit at night and relax,
While listening to my favourite tracks.

2.
The most wondrous thing just happened today,
When I was given a bonus of triple pay.

Bookmark Benchmark

I have an encyclopaedia on my bookshelf, made up of four volumes as shown in the picture. They're arranged so that the writing is the correct way up in each volume, and the spines are correctly labelled as shown.

I decide that I really want to become more educated, so I vow to read every page from the first page of the A–G book all the way through to the last page of the S–Z book.

In order to keep things varied, I decide to read from both the start and end of the encyclopaedia at the same time, so I place a bookmark next to the first page of the A–G book and a bookmark next to the last page of the S–Z book.

Given that each book is ten centimetres wide, roughly how far apart on my bookshelf are the two bookmarks? Don't worry about the width of the book covers.

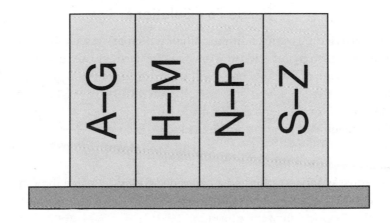

- You can see from the picture where each book is situated on the shelf. Doesn't that make calculating the distance quite easy, given that they are all ten centimetres wide?

- Think about where you would start reading in the first book, and where you would finish reading in the last book. So where would the bookmarks be on the shelf?

- The question mentions that all the books have the writing on the spine the same way up relative to the content, and that the spine labels are correct – why bother saying this?

Bookmark Benchmark
Puzzle 77 – Solutions

They would be twenty centimetres apart. We know that the books are stacked so that the writing inside is the correct way up, so the first page of the A–G book will be on the right-hand side of the book as we look at it on the shelf. Conversely, the last page of the S–Z book will be on the left-hand side as we look at the shelf. That means that only the widths of the H–M and N–R books come between them, *not* the A–G and S–Z books!

If the books were stacked with the writing upside down then this would not be true, which is why this is explicitly mentioned in the first paragraph of the question.

What the Dickens?

Puzzle 78 – Expert

Black out some of the words in this extract from *A Tale of Two Cities*, so what's left forms a very short story or passage of your own invention. You can even black out parts of words if you like, although it's entirely up to you. The idea is just to be creative.

In England, there was scarcely an amount of order and protection to justify much national boasting. Daring burglaries by armed men, and highway robberies, took place in the capital itself every night; families were publicly cautioned not to go out of town without removing their furniture to upholsterers' warehouses for security; the highwayman in the dark was a City tradesman in the light, and, being recognised and challenged by his fellow-tradesman whom he stopped in his character of "the Captain," gallantly shot him through the head and rode away; the mail was waylaid by seven robbers, and the guard shot three dead, and then got shot dead himself by the other four, "in consequence of the failure of his ammunition:" after which the mail was robbed in peace; that magnificent potentate, the Lord Mayor of London, was made to stand and deliver on Turnham Green, by one highwayman, who despoiled the illustrious creature in sight of all his retinue; prisoners in London gaols fought battles with their turnkeys, and the majesty of the law fired blunderbusses in among them, loaded with rounds of shot and ball; thieves snipped off diamond crosses from the necks of noble lords at Court drawing-rooms; musketeers went into St. Giles's, to search for contraband goods, and the mob fired on the musketeers, and the musketeers fired on the mob, and nobody thought any of these occurrences much out of the common way. In the midst of them, the hangman, ever busy and ever worse than useless, was in constant requisition; now, stringing up long rows of miscellaneous criminals; now, hanging a housebreaker on Saturday who had been taken on Tuesday; now, burning people in the hand at Newgate by the dozen, and now burning pamphlets at the door of Westminster Hall; to-day, taking the life of an atrocious murderer, and to-morrow of a wretched pilferer who had robbed a farmer's boy of sixpence.

If you're not sure how to begin, just pick some words to cross out or leave in, and see where you end up! Here's an example, just to show how it works:

In England, ~~there was scarcely an amount of order and protection to justify much national~~ boasting. ~~During burglaries by armed men, and highway robberies, took place in the capital itself every night;~~ families were ~~publicly cautioned not to go out of town without~~ removing their furniture ~~to upholsterers' warehouses for security; the highwayman~~ in the dark ~~was a City tradesman in the light, and, being recognised~~ and ~~challenged by his fellow-tradesman whom he stopped in his character of "the Captain," gallantly~~ shot ~~him through the head and rode away;~~ ~~the mail was waylaid by seven~~ robbers, ~~and the guard shot three~~ dead, ~~and then got shot dead himself by the other four, "in consequence of the failure of his ammunition:"~~ after ~~which the mail was robbed in~~ peace; ~~that magnificent potentate, the Lord Mayor of London,~~ was made ~~to stand and deliver~~ on ~~Turnham Green, by~~ one ~~highwayman, who despoiled the illustrious~~ creature in sight of ~~all his retinue; prisoners in~~ London ~~gaols fought battles with their turnkeys~~, and ~~the majesty of the law~~ fired ~~blunderbusses in among them, loaded with rounds of shot and ball;~~ thieves ~~snipped~~ off ~~diamond~~ crosses ~~from the necks of noble lords at~~ Court ~~drawing-rooms;~~ musketeers went ~~into St. Giles's, to search for contraband goods,~~ and ~~the mob~~ fired on ~~the musketeers, and the musketeers fired on the mob, and nobody thought any of these occurrences much out of~~ the common ~~way. In the midst of them, the hangman, ever busy and ever worse than useless, was in constant requisition, now, stringing up long rows of miscellaneous~~ criminals; ~~now, hanging a housebreaker on Saturday who had been taken on Tuesday; now,~~ burning people in ~~the hand at Newgate by the dozen, and now burning pamphlets at the door of~~ Westminster Hall; ~~to-day, taking the life of an atrocious murderer, and to-morrow~~ of a wretched ~~pilferer who had robbed a farmer's boy of~~ sixpence.

Tertiary Sequencing
Puzzle 79 – Expert

Can you work out which letter comes next in each of these real-world sequences?

For example, M T W T F S would be followed by 'S', since the sequence is Monday, Tuesday, Wednesday, Thursday, Friday, Saturday and then 'S' for Sunday.

1
W H T Q F S S

2
M D C L X V

Tertiary Sequencing
Puzzle 79 – Hints

1

- You'll definitely know this sequence.

- If you've solved the previous two sequence puzzle pages in this book, you should have an advantage!

2

- You'll know this sequence, even if you aren't precisely certain of all of the letters in it. You will definitely be able to work out which letter comes next, however, once you spot what it is.

- Try thinking back a bit. A really long bit. Say thousands of years.

Tertiary Sequencing
Puzzle 79 – Solutions

1
The next letter is 'E', since the sequence is fractions in increasing size of the denominator: whole, half, third, quarter, fifth, sixth, seventh and then finally 'E' for eighth.

2
The next letter is 'I', since the sequence is Roman numerals in decreasing order of value: M (1,000), D (500), C (100), L (50), X (10), V (5) and then finally I (1).

1

My mother recently gave me a pair of cufflinks
that she inherited from her father, and I happen
to know that a different mother also gave a
pair of inherited cufflinks to her child.

There is only one pair of cufflinks in
total, however, so how can this be?

———————

2

I recently had dinner with my niece, as did
my sister. And yet my sister's nephew is
not my nephew. How can this be true?

1

Does this sound like something that might happen in real life? If so, what is the rather mundane explanation in that case?

2

Try drawing a family tree if you have trouble thinking about this.

1

The second mother was me, and I passed the cufflinks I just inherited on to my child.

2

My sister's nephew is in this case my son.

You have a container that is full to the brim with exactly ten litres of water, but you wish to measure out precisely eight litres for a particular task.

You don't have any measuring containers, or indeed any other way of measuring the water, other than two empty containers whose exact volumes are three and seven litres.

You also have a funnel which allows you to pour liquid between containers without spilling any.

How can you measure out *precisely* eight litres of water? There is an exact solution to find – doing it 'by eye' is not the solution!

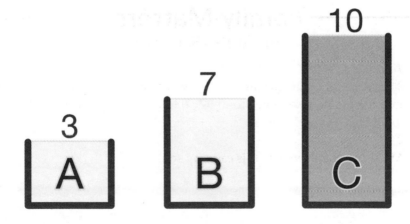

Water Worry

- It's going to take quite a few steps to measure out eight litres, so don't give up too quickly!

- Look for steps which allow you to measure out new quantities that you haven't previously made.

- First, try to measure out four litres in B.

- Now in a couple more steps you can measure nine litres into C.

- At this point, can you measure five litres in B?

- With five litres, and a three litre container, you're close.

Water Worry

Puzzle 81 – Solutions

Pour C into B for 0-7-3; B into A for 3-4-3; A into C for 0-4-6; B into A for 3-1-6; A into C for 0-1-9; B into A for 1-0-9; C into B for 1-7-2; B into A for 3-5-2; A into C for 0-5-5; B into A for 3-2-5; A into C for 0-2-8, solving the puzzle.

1

A man is having a face-to-face conversation with his friend, and he can clearly read a clock in the room over the shoulder of his friend which shows that the time is 4.30 p.m. At that moment, they both hear the 4.00 p.m. chimes of a church clock.

Both the church clock and the clock in the room are showing the correct time.

How can this be?

2

I take my watch to the jeweller to be repaired, but when I get it back there is something wrong with it. When the time should be 3.30 it shows 6.15, and when it should be 4.45 it shows 9.20.

What is wrong with the watch?

Timing Issues
Puzzle 82 – Hints

1

- Are there different types of, or ways to have, a face-to-face conversation?

- Why might two clocks with different times on both be simultaneously correct?

2

- What sort of watch might I have?

- Try putting down what you think the watch face would look like on paper. Is there some simple way you can see for this problem to occur?

Timing Issues
Puzzle 82 – Solutions

1

The friends are talking over a video chat link, and can hear and see each other. The man with the 4.30 p.m. clock is in Venezuela, which is four and a half hours behind GMT. The other man is in Washington DC, where the time is five hours behind GMT. So both clocks are correct.

2

The hands have been reversed on the analogue watch when they were reconnected, so the big hand points where the little hand should and vice-versa.

Puzzle 83 – Expert

At first glance, each of the images at the bottom of this page appears to be rather basic. The first is just some angled paths, and the second is some lines of varying thickness. But with a bit of imagination they can become something else.

You can even explain an empty box:

A polar bear in the dark

What creative descriptions can you come up with for each of the following images? There is space beneath each one to write a suitable caption!

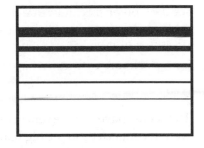

- If you aren't sure where to start, try and think of something each image genuinely looks like as a starting point.

- For example, the first image could be a close-up of a Christmas jumper pattern.

- The second image might be a frame from a 1980s music video!

Tales of the Unexplained
Puzzle 83 – Solutions

There's no correct answer here, of course.

For the first picture, how about two rows of tents erected in a field?

For the second picture, perhaps it is a line of tall posts running away from you, viewed from the ground when lying on your side?

Riddles to Reason

Puzzle 84 – Expert

1

Sometimes I'm bound,
Or even passed around,
And people get buried in me.
I open up, and then you see,
I sometimes can astound.
What am I?

—————

2

I open up and let you in,
Then you discard me with a fling.
You leave me lying in a hole,
Where I twist and rock and roll.
You first met me with a ring.
What am I?

1

- What is typically bound?

- What can you get 'buried in', metaphorically speaking?

2

- What might you leave in a hole?

- What can 'open up and let you in'?

1

A book, which you can 'get buried in', and which when you open it up and read it can sometimes astound.

2

A key, which will open a door and let you in, yet is often then lying in a (key)hole. You will often need to twist and rock it before rolling it, and when you first receive it you often put it on a ring.

Hidden View

Look at this empty square. It's hiding most of this picture, so you can just see parts of it sticking out on all four sides.

What do you think is *behind* the square? Grab a pencil, and draw in what you think might be concealed.

There's no correct answer, so it's impossible to get this puzzle 'wrong'!

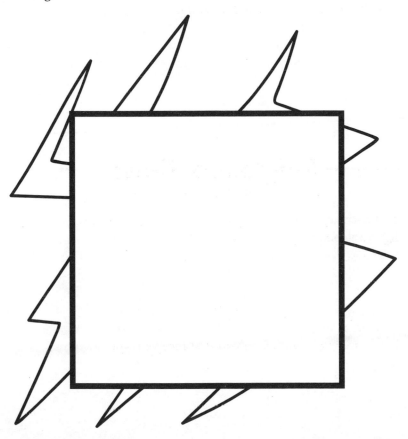

Hidden View

Puzzle 85 – Hints

- Are those insect limbs, maybe – is it a contorted grasshopper?

- Is it a bunch of boomerangs lying on the ground, perhaps?

- Is it a stylized cartoon character?

Hidden View

Puzzle 85 – Solutions

There's no correct solution, but maybe it's just a view of some lightning bolts?

Reservoir Reasoning
Puzzle 86 – Expert

You've been hired as a surveyor at a theme park, and the park owners want to renovate an existing water flume ride.

The ride involves a number of sections, all fed via a large underlying reservoir of water that continually pumps the water around the system to keep the flume ride running.

It's important that they have a good estimate of the volume of water used in the flume ride, but there are no existing records so you will need to work out the volume yourself.

The ride is far too large and complex to take accurate measurements of the depth and surface area throughout the ride, either via hand measurement or any kind of technological solution. Instead you will need to find another method to accurately estimate it.

No water flows in or out of the flume ride system, and you aren't permitted to drain it.

There is a reasonable method you can use to estimate the volume of water, but what is it?

- The ride is too complex to measure throughout, so you can't estimate the volume just by looking at it. You're going to have to interact with it in some way.

- No water can flow in or out of the ride system, and you can't drain it, so you can't measure the volume via any method that might involve that.

- Is there something you can add to the ride to help?

- Displacing the water is not the solution – there is far too much water in the ride and this would simply end up draining it, which is not allowed.

Reservoir Reasoning
Puzzle 86 – Solutions

You pour a known quantity of a harmless chemical marker into the water, and leave it time to disperse throughout the ride. Because the water is continually pumped around the ride, you can expect it to be reasonably well mixed-in throughout.

Now you take samples of the water throughout the ride and measure the volume of the marker found in each sample, which you then average. This will give you an estimate of its dilution, from which you can work out how much water is in the ride simply by multiplying up from the original volume of the chemical marker.

A Sweet Problem
Puzzle 87 – Expert

Anthea has a large, black jar of sweets that she received for her birthday. She is anxious not to lose any of them to her thieving brothers, so she decides to keep a 'sweet journal' to keep track of how many she has taken from the jar and how many remain.

She starts off with 40 sweets in her jar, and each day she reaches in and grabs a handful of sweets out of the jar then retires to her room to eat them and fill out her journal. After five days it looks like this:

Day	Sweets I ate today	Sweets remaining
Monday	20	20
Tuesday	10	10
Wednesday	4	6
Thursday	3	3
Friday	2	1
	Total = 39	**Total = 40**

As she writes in the results for Friday and works out the totals she screams out in anger – she has eaten one less sweet than the 40 in the jar, and yet she sees she has now accounted for all of the remaining sweets!

She runs off to accuse her brothers, but they all plead ignorance of the missing sweet.

As it turns out, her brothers are telling the truth. What has actually happened?

A Sweet Problem

- Do the figures all add up correctly, and are the subtractions from the amount remaining all correct too?

- This is a child's sweet ledger – is she doing all of her sums correctly?

- What would you see if you glanced at the outside of the jar without looking in?

- And what would you see if you looked down inside the jar?

- Are you sure the calculations make sense?

A Sweet Problem

What has happened is that Anthea has added up a column that is meaningless. The total number of sweets remaining in the jar is simply the number left in the jar itself; adding up the number of sweets remaining each day is meaningless.

Suppose that she had only taken one sweet each day, then this total after the fifth day would have been 39+38+37+36+35 = 185. It's simply coincidence that the total in this case happens to be 40.

The black jar that she is grabbing sweets out of means that she might easily not have seen that there is still one sweet remaining, since it's only when looking directly down inside that it's visible.

Torch Trouble

Four people are on an overnight trek.

Unfortunately, due to a lack of planning, they only have one torch between the four of them. When walking across fields this hasn't been much of a problem because they've simply stuck to the path, but now they have arrived at a rickety rope bridge.

The bridge has a number of missing slats, so they will need to use the torch when crossing. However, the bridge is only large enough to permit two people to cross over the bridge at once, so they must cross in pairs and then one person must come back each time with the torch.

The four people don't all walk at the same speed, and take the following lengths of time to cross the bridge:

- Andrew takes eight minutes to cross the bridge.

- Beatrice takes five minutes to cross the bridge.

- Charlie takes two minutes to cross the bridge.

- Daniella takes one minute to cross the bridge.

In order to share the torch, any pair crossing the bridge must cross at the speed of the slowest person in the pair.

Find a strategy that lets all four people cross to the other side in just fifteen minutes.

Torch Trouble
Puzzle 88 – Hints

- It's tempting to have the fastest person cross back with the torch each time, but with that method they'll end up taking seventeen minutes to cross the bridge. If you aren't sure why it's seventeen minutes, write out the various stages and add up the times.

- Now how can you change the strategy to let them all cross in a shorter period of time?

Torch Trouble
Puzzle 88 – Solutions

The secret is to have the slowest people cross together, and then neither of them cross back, so that the most 'expensive' part of the journey, in terms of time spent, is minimized. Therefore a possible solution is as follows:

Have Charlie and Daniella cross the bridge, taking 2 minutes.
Have Daniella cross back, taking 1 minute.
Have Andrew and Beatrice cross over, taking 8 minutes.
Have Charlie cross back, taking 2 minutes.
Have Charlie and Daniella cross the bridge, taking 2 minutes.

Total time = 15 minutes. Problem solved!

Coin Revolution

Imagine that you have two of the same coin on a table or other flat surface. Now imagine that you place them flat down on the table so that they touch but don't overlap.

If you were to now press down on one coin so that it can't move, and then slowly roll the other coin all the way around the outside of that first coin, how many revolutions about its own axis would the moving coin make?

Assume that the coins make perfect contact with each other all the way around.

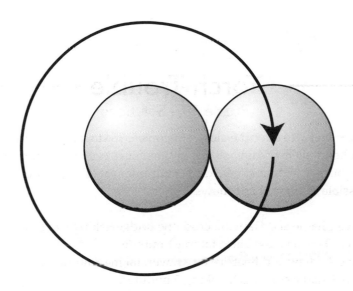

Coin Revolution

- Both coins have the same circumference, so on the face of it you might imagine that the coin will only make one revolution. But you'd be wrong!

- You need to allow for the rotary motion of the second coin, compared to the static nature of the first coin. So the second coin will travel further than just one length of its own circumference.

- It can be hard to imagine this, so why not get two coins and give it a go?

Coin Revolution

The coin will perform exactly two revolutions on its way around the coin you're holding still. If you're not convinced, give it a go! You'll need to push the second coin reasonably firmly against the first as you rotate it, to ensure it doesn't slip at all.

You should see it make one full revolution as it travels halfway around the first coin, and then of course a second full revolution during the remainder of its journey.

A Final Cut
Puzzle 90 – Expert

For this challenge you'll need a square of paper and a pair of scissors. A small sheet from a memo block is ideal, or otherwise you can simply cut a rectangular sheet of paper into a rough square. You don't need a large sheet of paper – in fact, pretty much any size will do.

The challenge is to reproduce a pattern *only* by repeatedly folding the paper in half, and then making a *single* straight line cut.

You can fold either diagonally or horizontally/vertically, just so long as the paper ends up being exactly half the size after the fold that it was before. The single cut, which is the final step, can be wherever you like, then unfold the paper. For example, you can form a rotated square in the centre of a piece of paper like this:

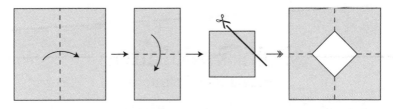

Now work out how to form this result by following these rules:

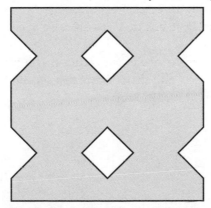

A Final Cut
Puzzle 90 – Hints

- To form the sixteen lines of these cut-outs you must fold four times – each fold will double the number of lines cut.

- The precise position of the squares will depend on where you make the final cut – the orientation of the cut matters.

- For angled squares you are probably going to cut a corner off, as in the example.

- Start by folding in half vertically.

- Now fold in half horizontally.

- Fold two more times and then make the cut.

A Final Cut
Puzzle 90 – Solutions

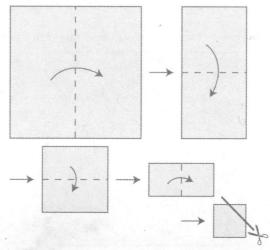